KU-572-156

GOOD
GRIEF

Also by Catherine Mayer:

Amortality: The Pleasures and Perils of Living Agelessly
Charles: The Heart of a King
Attack of the 50 Ft. Women: How Gender Equality Can
Save The World!

GOOD GRIEF

Embracing life at a time of death

CATHERINE MAYER
AND ANNE MAYER BIRD

ONE PLACE. MANY STORIES

HQ
An imprint of HarperCollins*Publishers* Ltd
1 London Bridge Street
London SE1 9GF

This edition 2020

1

First published in Great Britain by
HQ, an imprint of HarperCollins*Publishers* Ltd 2020

Copyright © Catherine Mayer and Anne Mayer Bird 2020

Catherine Mayer and Anne Mayer Bird assert the moral right to be
identified as the authors of this work.
A catalogue record for this book is
available from the British Library.

HB ISBN: 978-0-00-843610-0
TPB ISBN: 978-0-00-843611-7

MIX
Paper from
responsible sources
FSC
www.fsc.org   FSC™ C007454

This book is produced from independently certified FSC™ paper
to ensure responsible forest management.

For more information visit: www.harpercollins.co.uk/green

This book is set in 11.7/16 pt. Sabon by Type-it AS, Norway

Printed and bound in Great Britain by
CPI Group (UK) Ltd, Croydon, CR0 4YY

All rights reserved. No part of this publication may be reproduced,
stored in a retrieval system, or transmitted, in any form or by any means,
electronic, mechanical, photocopying, recording or otherwise,
without the prior permission of the publishers.

This book is sold subject to the condition that it shall not, by way of trade
or otherwise, be lent, re-sold, hired out or otherwise circulated without
the publisher's prior consent in any form of binding or cover other than
that in which it is published and without a similar condition including this
condition being imposed on the subsequent purchaser.

To Andy and John, with our undying love

Contents

Introduction

We are extraordinarily lucky, my mother and I. We have each other and we have this room.

When she and John moved to London, married just three years and still figuring out the shape of their relationship, their new home had not yet established its boundaries either. The room came later. At first the house grew warily, adding a small glass extension at the back with a slippery incline that their ginger cat treated as a slide. The local foxes chose a bigger playing field, barking and tumbling on the flat roof of the builders' merchant abutting the property, a comparatively recent arrival to this estate of Victorian townhouses. The neighbourhood had seen wealthier days and would do so again. Nothing stays the same, no matter how solid it appears.

In a portent of gentrification, developers made plans to demolish the commercial unit next door and build, in its stead, a new house made to look old. My mother and stepfather debated what to do. They had more than enough space already. Yet they feared that a new neighbour, sharing a party wall, might prove noisy and, anyway, John wanted somewhere to put a piano and the art that he had started to make and collect. After five decades working in jobs he didn't much enjoy ('a lifetime,' he said, though it proved to be just three-fifths of his total

I

Leabharlanna Poiblí Chathair Baile Átha Cliath
Dublin City Public Libraries

span), he retired and began to reinvent himself as a painter. They bought the unit and knocked through the party wall, creating for themselves a garage, utility area, extra bathroom, and this, a cavernous second living room.

If truth be told – and the conversations my mother and I conduct in this room often worm out truths unknown to either or both of us until the moment of utterance – I never until recently warmed to this room. Its industrial proportions make it a perfect place to display paintings or throw big parties. It is less successful as a venue for intimate discussions. Two big armchairs maintain a chilly distance against the far wall, acknowledging each other only with a slight angling that directs the gaze of any occupants towards the centre of the room and, beyond that emptiness, to a Chesterfield at the opposite wall.

This is where my tiny mother usually sits, Thumbelina on the full-sized sofa, during our weekly meetings. After John died and my husband Andy stunned us by following suit forty-one days later, she and I saw each other often but at varying intervals. It was the lockdown against coronavirus, coming seven weeks after Andy's death, that enforced on our timetable a form and regularity. New government rules to combat the unfolding pandemic isolated us in our fresh isolation, my mother who had never in her eighty-six years lived on her own and me, alone again after twenty-nine years of coalescence. Only when Andy had gone did I realise how much he and I resembled a sight we often stopped to admire on our weekend walks, a tree and railing merged into a single entity, the tree enfolding, the railing sustaining.

Exposed now and unsupported, I looked for fresh ways to hold myself up. The imperative to help out my mother came not as a burden, but like the small services I performed for others in those early lockdown days – supplying food and medicine, posting parcels – as a gift. In doing these things, I found the iron necessary to stay upright. More than that, my Sunday visits to my mother, legitimate under the rules as care work, provided the only meaningful face-to-face interactions I would have during that period, even if the lower halves of our faces were masked.

Even now it continues. Every second Sunday I change her duvet. Most weeks I fix (or try to fix) something, an iPad one visit, a recalcitrant filing cabinet the next. Every week I bring meals I've prepared to her requests (cauliflower cheese was an early favourite; latterly we've been exploring curries). There are often other items to source too: shoes, hanging files, birthday cards. She presents me with a to-do list when I arrive – she calls it an 'agenda' – and we work through it. Then, at the end of my visit, we allow ourselves to relax, she on the sofa, me in one of the safely distant chairs. And we talk.

Our starting point is usually a piece of news from the past week, whether small and personal or global and transformative. These things are anyway linked in unexpected ways. In the first months, our battles to persuade service providers to transfer household accounts into our names dragged on as the virus and furlough schemes depleted staff numbers. Automated systems failed the easiest of tests. 'How can I help you today, Andrew?' 'I'm Andrew's widow. Andrew is dead.' 'Oh dear, Andrew, that doesn't sound good.'

For the worst part of the past year, Facebook has shown me advertisements for funeral services, as if the mischance that saw me notifying John's friends of his death in December, organising his exequies at Golders Green Crematorium in January, Andy's cremation at the same venue on Valentine's Day and his memorial at the beginning of March, bespeaks a delicious new pastime. The same algorithms that take me for a funeral hobbyist decide which posts are seen by whom, which propaganda to channel to voters. They may have helped install the populist leaders in the US, Brazil and here in the UK who responded to Covid-19 not with life-saving policies but bluster and blarney.

In the big room with its gallery of paintings, the weekly meetings with my mother unfold against another, grim backdrop, both strange and horribly familiar. As the global toll of the virus rises, we cannot help but understand each death not as a statistic but a sequence of events, a body shutting down, the person there and then not there, never again there, the families distraught and numb, embarking on the same path that we already tread.

Bereavement is an odd phenomenon, full of twists and surprises, nasty ambushes and unexpected dark humour. It is the little things that knock you off course. I work dry-eyed through snowdrifts of 'sadmin', but weep when the wifi conks out. One day I call the funeral director to pay by credit card for Andy's cremation. The man in the accounts department runs through the usual drill: name, credit card number, expiry date. For a second I genuinely don't know whether he means for the card or my beloved. Laughter, inappropriate and all the harder to control for that fact, wells up. The man takes my thickened voice as a sign of grief. For days afterwards, I find myself sniggering.

We are aware, my mother and I, that we discomfit well-wishers. Most people are scared to death of death and unsure how to talk about it, yet curiously our composure unnerves them more than tears. We appear functional and less fragile than they expect. Might our similar reactions and coping mechanisms point to universalities about grief and loss or to the specifics of our family's history and culture? We don't know, but assume a mixture of both. As a child, my mother lost her father and brother in quick succession. When my sisters and I were children, the stepfather she loved took his own life.

These experiences surely shaped her and her parenting, informing my own conspicuous self-sufficiency, which Andy sometimes found difficult. (Oh, my love, if only you knew how much I need you.) A run of deaths among those closest to me from my thirties onwards, excluding John and Andy, four alone in the past four years, prepared me for widowhood in two significant ways: I already knew grief to be as mobile as a cat on a cantilevered glass roof and I already knew that the lovely dead never leave us. If we learn not to flinch from the pain, the lovely dead enfold us, tree to railing.

It is because of this knowledge, accrued and unasked for, that I agreed to write this book. You cannot be proofed against grief. You can be prepared for it, for the inevitability of loss and the screeching arrival of its outriders: disruption, despair and dread tape, the red tape of death. Our culture, in recoiling from death, medicalising it, shoving it behind screens and banning it from polite conversation, does us no favours. For too many, those horsemen come as a nasty surprise, wringing from their targets an anguished 'good grief!'. My mother and I aspire in sharing our experiences to imbue that cartoon phrase with a different, and constructive, meaning.

Even so, we do not address you in this book from a position of lofty authority. The subject isn't new to me. I've lost too many people and I also wrote, some years back, a book called *Amortality* that examined the phenomenon of widespread denial not only of death but ageing. Yet such expertise as my mother and I will share with you derives less from research than from the frontline of our own emotions and experiences. We are recent widows, open and vulnerable. Our equanimity is a front, a construct, that we must believe, with time, will add layers and substance. We are allergic to the question 'And how are you?', especially if delivered in a sorrow-laden voice, the inquisitor's head tilted to the side. How should we reply when the answer changes by the hour or do so honestly without resurfacing feelings we have struggled to subdue? The doctrine of letting it all hang out, crying as catharsis, may work for some people. To my mother and me, it brings no relief. For now we aim for functionality rather than intensity. As we will explain later in these pages, you have to relearn how to be before you relearn how to live.

If not for lockdown, we could seek solace from the company of family and friends, hang out, speak if we wished, stay silent if we preferred, talk of important things or TV shows. We can never replace the cradling we miss the most, but we could hug and be hugged. In the eleventh week of lockdown, as I queue for bread, a man walks into me with force and intent. At first all I can think is how angry he is. I realise later that this is the first and only human touch I've experienced not just since lockdown, but from the start of social distancing.

Mother's Day has fallen, with cruel precision, on the eve of lockdown. Boris Johnson reveals during a press conference that he hopes to celebrate with his 77-year-old mum; Downing Street later 'clarifies' his remarks to say he means to Skype her. My sisters and I decide on one last visit together to our mother, in her living room, embracing not her but its edges. It is already decided that I will be the only one of us during lockdown to cross her threshold. My middle sister Lise will lock down with her son. My eldest sister, Cassie, and stepsister Catherine A are key workers. Cassie, as duty manager of a municipal stable, is responsible with a small team for keeping eighty-eight horses fed, watered and, in the enforced absence of clients, exercised. Catherine A teaches.

(A quick side note here: memoirs, by their nature, are messy, the contents shaped not for ease of storytelling but by random circumstances. When they married, my mother and John created a family of five daughters, two called Catherine. To avoid confusion, my mother and I refer to my stepsister Catherine in this book by her first name and the initial A for Anderson, her surname through marriage.)

My siblings' commitments mean they have less flexibility than I and more exposure to potential virus-carriers. It is safest for me, alone as I am, to be my mother's designated carer, not that she would recognise herself or our relationship in that phrase. She is right. I depend on her just as much as she on me.

During this last family gathering before lockdown, she looks smaller than usual. As the conversation moves on to how we will fill our time, Cassie suggests that she should write. At this stage everyone imagines, wrongly, that lockdown promises reams of hours, as empty and full of potential as blank pages. My mother started writing a memoir when she was 11, *What Makes My Childhood Fun*, gave it up with the death of her father a year later. Recently she resumed the project as an adult, picking up from her early years and continuing into the first part of her marriage to our father. She would send us chapters, fascinating, engaging, sometimes a little unsettling. For her eighty-fifth birthday, Lise had the chapters bound into a book.

In March, a friend from her neighbourhood asks her to start contributing to a website aimed at women over fifty. The words burst out. The new blogger has so much to say, not least about the ways in which older generations are simultaneously patronised and unprotected, instructed to shield and left to die as Covid rips through care homes. The website prefers positive angles, so she exhorts readers to reject reductive ideas about age, drawing on her own experiences and routines as examples. The beneficiary of good genes, exercise and an adult life without significant economic struggles, she remains fiercely active, working, until the virus shuttered theatres, as a freelance publicist. One day I offer to perform a small chore for her. 'Oh good,' she says. 'I'll use the time to do my staircase walking.' It turns out she walks up and down her staircase thirty times a day.

Her blogs are good, but they conceal as much as they reveal, an extension of the brave face she turns to the world, its scarlet lipstick applied every morning. There is another woman behind the bravado who longs and aches. On 27 March, ninety-six days after John dies, that woman sits down and writes to him, the first of a series of letters about the events that have roiled our family and the world since he died. In writing to and for my stepfather, my mother lets her defences fall. She writes as if he could answer. She writes without filter.

Until Andy died, I could write that way too. For most of my life, writing had been not just the way I made a living but the way that I lived. Often I would not be sure what I thought or felt until the process of writing gave me clarity. As a journalist and non-fiction author, I immersed myself in research. Writing, like a sculptor's tools, revealed the shape within the marble. I also wrote for myself, poems and stories and, in the months leading up to Andy's death, fifty thousand horribly prescient words of a novel, set in a world scarred by a pandemic, about a woman who loses to death the love of her life.

When, at the start of lockdown, my friend Jo messaged me: 'Tell me you ARE writing a book about these weirdest of grief-blurred days...', I told her, no. I couldn't write, but for the eulogy – in the truest sense of the word – that poured forth, without pause or revision, one bleak pre-dawn. Two days earlier, I had watched my love die, twelve minutes between the unhooking of the machines and the extinction of all hope. I would read the eulogy, unchanged, at his memorial. After writing it, I shut the laptop and closed down, though I didn't realise this at the time. The world had closed down too. In the sensory deprivation of lockdown, untouched and sequestered, no sounds in the flat or outside on the streets but for Thursday nights when we clapped for the NHS that had tried and failed to save him, I lost the connection between words, thoughts and feelings.

It is either coincidence or a measure of how closely bound my mother and I have become that the day I recovered that facility was 27 March. As she composed the first of her letters to John, I set up a new blog, *2020 Vision*, on my website and wrote, intimately, about Andy's death. My conscious reason for doing so was to stave off all those unwanted *And how are yous?* By answering the question in more detail than anyone asking could possibly wish, making public my innermost thoughts, I sought to preserve my privacy.

I also hoped to scotch rumours about Andy. Perhaps two hours after he died, as I sat with his band members in the atrium of the critical care unit that had been our assembly point for that final week, journalists began calling me for quotes and to ask questions about the manner of his death. The next morning, one of his fans somehow procured my phone number and rang, weeping, looking to me for comfort. As I begged him please not to call again, he interrupted. There was something he must know: what really killed Andy? The internet did its thing too, embroidering the fact that Andy's band, Gang of Four, had toured in China in November 2019 into a dark tale of Covid and cover-up.

It was true that after Andy's admission to St Thomas's on 18 January, doctors had asked about his travels, briefly considering whether he might have contracted the novel coronavirus that even now locked down Wuhan, but the timelines, as we then knew them, appeared to rule this out. 'He did not, as online conspiracists allege, die from Covid-19,' I wrote in that first blog, 'but he had an underlying condition, sarcoidosis, that would have put him at high risk. The immunosuppressants he took to manage it laid him open to the pneumonia that proved implacable. He did not die from Covid-19 but his death, in many details, resembled that of a Covid-19 fatality, respiratory failure, the battle to keep him alive long enough to give him a chance of life.' Later I would question that assertion, and begin to investigate, to contemplate dreadful possibilities. This is a story I also tell in this book, not least because it has to be told. If Andy had in fact been killed by Covid, then the timelines and basis for the public health response were wrong. There was a sharply personal realisation too, that John – officially the victim of 'hospital-acquired pneumonia' – might also have succumbed to it, one of many thousands of Covid dead unrecognised in official statistics.

This thought, I was aware, would destabilise my mother and not just for the obvious reason that it would force her to revisit John's death. Something odd happens when the person you love most in the world dies: all at once they are nowhere and everywhere, absent and omnipresent. Andy, essence of Andy, Andyness permeates every aspect of my life, every action and interaction. He is in the cutlery drawer, in its unfeasibly large collection of implements for opening oysters. He is, as you would expect, in the music studio in our basement. He is in every bar of soap in the flat, not one of them bought, all nicked from hotel bathrooms, a habit he picked up from touring. He is in the wardrobe, on a shelf holding hundreds of pairs of identical slimline underpants. A market stall near our house sold these cheaply and Andy, for unfathomable reasons, reacted like a shopper during a pandemic, stockpiling those pants.

This Andy is gloriously flawed. He has not yet been polished by the abrasions of time, sanitised and reworked to inhuman perfection by the human desire to remember the best of the lovely dead. This is the Andy I aim to keep around for as long as I can, and those first days after he dies make clear just how difficult this will be. Questions about Covid, at this stage, aren't persistent, but interest is. He is a public figure, all the more so in death. Across the world, he prompts banner headlines, makes the early evening news, then the next bulletin and the next and the next, well into the following day. He trends, for twenty-four hours, on Twitter. Then come the obituaries, some good, some sloppy, all of them telling me, telling all of us, 'this is who Andy was'.

I knew instinctively to resist my own impulse to selective memory, but hadn't realised how many alternative Andys would challenge mine. Nor could I ignore the impact on my mother and the rest of the family. Barely had my sisters and I gathered around my mother, sought ways to support her in her new widowhood, than we were pulled away, to Andy's bedside and thence into the depths of our grief. My mother lost and kept losing. She loved Andy, too, so much so that I used to tease her about it. In my eulogy for Andy – reproduced in full later in this book – I mentioned an invitation she once sent to both of us, addressed to 'Andy Gill plus one'.

Alive, Andy's charisma could relegate me to my mother's afterthought. In death, he shadowed and overshadowed her agony, risked blunting and blurring memories of John. My stepfather was a big character, genial, complex, interested in everything, still making up for time lost to a career in sales, first tyres then insurance, that suppressed his curiosity and creativity. His love for my mother was prodigious and hers for him unquestionable, as was clear the moment I first saw them together, forty-something years ago. He was 83 when he died, but still only in the foothills of his ambitions, for himself and, more than that, for others. People remembered him not just as a family member, friend or colleague but as someone who changed their lives for the better. When the noise and anguish around Andy cut across all this love and loss, I worried for my mother, for all this could mean.

She would tell you herself – she will tell you herself in these pages – that these fears were justified, but that together we found ways to navigate our mutual and intersecting grief and to hold on to the Andyness, the Johnness and our shredded hearts. In this room, this living room, we are learning to embrace the things we can't touch, each other and the lovely dead.

We hope in sharing our insights and learnings to help those of you who have lost or will lose people you love or who wish to know how best to support others in such circumstances. We don't pretend to have all the answers or even all the questions, but we believe we can impart at least a few essential examples of both. Death has been having a busy time of it, dashing from one household to the next like a malign Santa Claus. We will talk about the additional challenges to grieving and coping during a pandemic, but most of what we discuss is not specific to this period or these circumstances. It is just that Covid has made these things visible. If humanity can drag any positives from this global tragedy, it will be in addressing the deep dysfunctions the virus uncovered. This book is not a manifesto for equality, though it touches, often, on the tragic consequences of inequality. Covid was never, despite the protestations of politicians, a leveller. On the contrary: it revealed the degree to which some lives are valued more highly than others and some deaths, as a result, disregarded. It also showed the manifold ways in which we are unprepared for the end of life and its aftermath.

Every one of us will die; every one of us will have to deal with death. The central purpose of this book is to make the inevitable better and more bearable.

To that end, although this is not in any sense a handbook, my mother and I seek to distil from our interwoven narratives key lessons not only about grief but about some of the practicalities of bereavement. My mother's narrative comes in the form of the letters she wrote to John and one she addressed to herself. This book came about after I showed her letters to my publisher, with no intention of writing anything myself. I had found in the letters resonances, learned to understand not just my mother's grief but my own, and in securing for them a wider audience, I hoped that they might help others in the same way.

In the end, I agreed to write too, about two much-missed men, their widows and a search for truth. In telling our story,

I aim to offer an antidote to the numbing effect of charts and undifferentiated death tolls, statistics and numbers. Every death matters because every life matters. This is a memoir of love and loss in the time of corona, of relearning to live in my mother's living room.

Please join us there.

Chapter 1: Loss

My mother held a party in her living room exactly a week before John died. She was beginning to grapple with a challenge that in pre-pandemic days still confronted the bereaved: how to recalibrate changed personal circumstances to an unchanged world. Life, but for the life that meant the most, would go on. The party gave her brief respite from this growing awareness and, in a small way, modelled a new idea of how she might live without John, alone but not isolated, buoyed by friends and family. She could not know that the virus would soon transform the world too, banishing from her living room all society but mine.

These days we play catch-up, we who are grieving. How should we reimagine our lives when everything around us is in flux? One answer, though not mine, is to follow the dictum of recovery programmes, to take one step at a time. You may find this approach helpful and it is certainly my mother's default. Throughout John's illness, she resisted giving much detailed thought to a future without him and instead got on with doing the things that were still possible. As a result, his last years were full of light and vibrancy. When he could no longer walk or breathe without external oxygen, she pushed him in a wheelchair. Though she be but little, she is fierce. They maintained a busy social life. She kept up a considerable workload free-lancing as an arts publicist and assisting a theatre company to stage a touring production; he painted. In December, however, ringed by fairy lights and festivities, worries crept through the cracks in her composure. How will I do the supermarket run, she wondered aloud. (John drove, she did not.) Who will cook when I entertain? (For years, John had done all the cooking.)

She still held out hope that John might be home for Christmas, not just the coming holiday but the one after that. They had married on 29 December 1980, and, as John's health deteriorated, she set her sights on celebrating their fortieth anniversary together. He encouraged this optimism, but never fully shared it; he knew he couldn't be at the drinks party, but chivvied her to go ahead with it. John recognised in my mother's focus on small things and increments of time a bottomless fear of something much bigger: losing him. He could cope with his own suffering and wanted to forestall hers.

It was a nice party, with five of their closest friends, and Andy and me, he on fine form, returned recently from a tour that had taken him to Australia, New Zealand, Japan and China. He wore an orange shirt and told vivid stories. Everyone mixed easily. The life my mother and John had built together was intensely sociable, blending different generations and strands from their long and variegated histories. After so many years, more than a few of their pleasures and passions had merged, though she ceded the telly to him when the rugby was on. Both knew what they liked and what, most definitely, they did not. They enjoyed parties and lunches and dinners, trips to the theatre and to galleries. They loathed inactivity and Conservativism.

John was given to declaring some of his deepest aversions

on Facebook. On 2 December, he had posted an article from the *Independent*; its headline: 'Boris Johnson says salary of £141,000 is "not enough to live on". He will have to learn to live within his means like the rest of us,' he commented. 'Poor boy. It might also help if he kept his zip done up when out with women and stopped creating more arseholes.'

The following morning, an ambulance collected him for a pre-arranged appointment at UCLH, a hospital where he was not only a patient but a former governor. For several years he also served in this voluntary capacity at Moorfields Eye Hospital. John believed in the NHS and in active citizenship. If you wanted a better world, you should help to build it.

He may have been relieved when UCLH decided to keep him in. His conditions – chronic obstructive pulmonary disease and a form of blood cancer – were incurable. Steroids to control the COPD had weakened his bones, too. In constant pain from spinal fractures and flares of cellulitis, dependent now not just on ambulatory oxygen but a large compressor that sat in the living room alongside the other paraphernalia of his illness, he might easily be mistaken for someone without joy or reason to go on. After he died, well-meaning friends would say that 'he had a good innings' or that 'it was his time' or even that his death came as 'a merciful release'.

The truth was more intricate. It always is. John loved life, loved my mother, still had things he wanted to do. The last place he wanted to be was in this hospital bed. If, as seemed entirely possible, he had more juice left in him, he wanted to come home, to live in the living room with its step-free access to a bathroom. This would require home care. He knew his medical needs had become too complex for my mother to manage on her own. He also looked on the process of dying much as he regarded Boris

Johnson, enraged by the fact and stupidity of it and wanting nothing so much as to see the back of it.

Only in that sense was John, at the end, ready to die. His last words, shouted suddenly at a knot of family talking animatedly and pulling him back to consciousness, were 'shut up'.

Sometimes it is better to keep quiet. There can be a lot of noise around loss, the rattle of hospital trolleys and crematoria conveyor belts, the empty phrases casting death as a blessing. Yet this is not, by any means, an injunction to avoid substantial conversations around death. One aim of this book is to equip you with a better understanding of how to have such conversations and the importance of doing so.

Twenty people close to me I've lost in the past twenty-seven years, eleven of whom, including John, I saw at or near the moment of extinction. Those who could still speak had last messages to impart. On the eve of his death, John instructed me to look after my mother; that same day he mentioned to her that she might find another partner. People often presume to speak for the dead. 'He would have wanted you to be happy,' they say. John wanted my mother to be happy. I know this because he told me.

The dying often discuss their own predicaments too, seeking not so much comfort as connection. This is helpful to understand, because those grating platitudes about death come from a place of good intention: we want to make the dying and the grieving feel better. It is the wrong ambition. What we should aim for, instead, is to support the dying and the grieving while death or time do their work.

That starts with being honest. I think of a family meal, already tinged with sadness. My stepsister Catherine A has fallen into the excellent custom, since the death of her older sister Sarah, of organising annual gatherings to mark what would have been Sarah's birthday. The last of these John attended took place an exact calendar month before he died and three days before Andy's return from China.

A surprise awaited John at Catherine A's house, a good one. He knew most of his grandchildren would be there, but hadn't expected to see Sarah's eldest, newly back from working in Germany. He chatted with her and with all of us. For much of the evening, he seemed himself, which is to say, convivial, interested, game for any conversation, undaunted by age gaps or the hubbub of people talking across each other. Our combined family is generously endowed with opinions and seldom reticent to share them. Andy sometimes found this wearing, but not John; on the contrary, John was always in the thick of it, the Duke of Debate, the Prince of Polemic, arguing his case, laughing, head thrown back with the joy of it all.

This evening, though, he began to flag, in pain and pained to be talked over in his chair. 'Oh for goodness sake,' he exclaimed suddenly. 'Don't you know that I'm dying?'

In that moment, he needed neither distraction nor soothing words, but recognition of his situation – and of his anger. Just one person I have ever seen greet death without a shred of resentment. Andy's Auntie June, at 92, yellowed with jaundice but comfortable, had lived with meaning and purpose; at this juncture she could no longer do so. Like John, if she must die, she wanted to get on with the business of dying. Her body's refusal to let go as fast as she would have liked was the trade-off for a robust constitution that had sustained her through world wars, social and cultural revolutions and repeated proofs of the human capacity to ignore the lessons of history.

Most everyone else whose ending I've witnessed railed against extinction, even when that outcome was inevitable and decline merciless. At 97, my paternal grandmother Jane resented the rude interruption to her plans, fighting death to the last. By the time cerebellar ataxia finished off my close friend Richard, just before his forty-eighth birthday, it had stripped him of control over movement, then of movement itself, of speech and of functional eyesight. Still, he dug in his heels. My stepsister Sarah might have been expected, as a committed Christian, to accept mortality easily, but her grace in meeting her fate could not mask the distress of being taken, aged 52, from daughters and a new husband, from a blossoming career in politics and an unfinished thesis.

Sarah died in October 2016. A month later, one of my best friends Sara Burns – I distinguish her from my stepsister by refer-ring to her in these pages as Sara B – finally succumbed to cancer too. She had survived melanoma in her thirties, then twenty years ago received the first of a series of breast cancer diagnoses, by chance in the same week a drug overdose killed another close friend. A short time later, Nicky, my best friend since university, while nursing her youngest child discovered a lump in her breast. It was not, as her GP assured her, a swollen milk gland, but cancer. She would survive, but suddenly I found myself alone among our friendship group to be whole of body if not in spirit.

Sixteen more years Sara B kept going, comforting me throughout that period as if I, not she, were in mortal danger. After a later diagnosis, finally at the edge of any therapies she could tolerate, she asked me to help her campaign for assisted dying. She did this not with a view to shortening her life but to enhancing the life she had left by freeing herself from the fear of a bad death. Maurice, my sister Cassie's close companion, and Barbara, my former editor and mentor, shared this perspective, and like Sara B died in protracted and painful ways. If help had been at hand to terminate their lives, they might have accepted it, but perhaps later in the process than they originally envisaged. Maurice in his final weeks still talked of projects he hoped to see through. Barbara starved herself to try to escape the last, agonising stanza, but right up to the point of taking such drastic action regretted that her life should be over. The cancer ate at Sara B's bones and seeded strange tumours, one, jutting below her clavicle, that pressed on her heart and lungs. No matter the pain, something – a will to live, a sense of potential – kept her fighting for ragged breath.

Where there's life, there's denial, a final bond between the dying and those who love them. Death breaks the compact, leaving the bereaved to face the truth alone. The stillness of a body is unarguable, non-negotiable. In that moment you understand the stories of the parents fighting in the courts to keep alive children for whom no life, in a meaningful sense, will ever be possible. In that moment you realise that there is a form of loneliness more profound than sitting by a bedside, listening to the mechanical breath of your sweetheart. You knew, intellectually, that there was no hope of a recovery, but you hoped for some kind of a reprieve. You would rather hold a warm, insensate hand than no hand at all.

For my mother, who at 12 saw her father fall dead, and less than a year later lost her only sibling, younger brother Kenny, to a lightning strike – a force so savage and sudden that it serves as its own metaphor – the prospect of watching John die was unbearable. She had limited tolerance for hospital visits even when she hoped to bring him home. After UCLH hung the sign of a swan at his door, signalling to staff his impending death and their changed medical priorities – comfort, peace and no unnecessary intervention – she left for the evening. My sisters and I kept watch over him in turn. Catherine A was with him when he died, quietly she said, an alteration almost imperceptible but equally unmistakable.

It was around 9 p.m. that this happened, a little later when Catherine A called. I was to let my mother know. I paused to tell Andy; he and John had bonded deeply over decades and the experience of holding their own within this family. Andy cried, then held me as I, also crying, rang my mother. She guessed the news as soon as she heard my voice, asked a few, leaden questions and rejected my offer to come over. She later explained that she had been watching an adaptation of *A Christmas Carol*. When she put down the receiver, she returned, numb, to the television to watch the rest of it. I'm not sure what she did for the rest of that night, whether she wept, whether she slept, whether she felt the sharpness of loss or the dull weight of blanketing shock. Certainly her small fears returned and multiplied in the coming days and weeks, no longer bypassing her defences but amalgamating to create a buzzing distraction from her underlying anguish.

My mother and I write elsewhere in this book about the administrative burden that attends every death and the unintended sting of the phrase that repeatedly drops from the lips of those intending comfort: 'It's good to be busy'. Oh no it isn't, not when that busyness consists of a daily battle with institutional incompetence and bureaucracy, compounded by apprehension about whether you can pay for the funeral, household utilities and basics, whether you can afford to stay put or might need to move. All these things we experienced, and we are the lucky ones, privileged, cushioned. We had assets to sell if we needed to, friends and family who offered to help out.

The only slender positive of dread tape and sadmin is that they occupy headspace that might otherwise brim with thoughts of giving up. So it was that my mother's campaign to retrieve John's Nectar points and add them to her own card preoccupied her during the aftermath of John's death and during Andy's final days. She informed Sainsbury's customer services of her aims; instead of assisting her, they suspended John's card. It took interventions by Cassie and by my mother herself to restore the points.

An outsider might have mistaken her focus for a lack of deeper feeling. How could she care about such a trivial matter when she had lost, so recently, her greatest love and must soon bid farewell to the son-in-law she cherished? The answer, of course, is that trivialities helped to divert her from considerations she could not, at that stage, endure. I grasped only when she began to write her post-mortem letters to John how much she had held in check. The contrast between those letters and the eulogy she wrote for John and asked me to read at his funeral is telling. Lovely though the eulogy was, it told their origin story, about how they met in a wine bar, a tale honed with years of repetition, about them but not, in any depth, about *him*. She was moved – we all were – by the more detailed tribute their friend Ian delivered at the funeral. It pleased her that he had so well understood and appreciated John. It would be many weeks before she could let herself fully access that understanding and appreciation, because to do so would also confront her with the scale of her loss.

My coping mechanism was different, a swift-onset, selective amnesia. Every minute of Andy's dying is etched in my memory, but the only reason I can tell you how I got home from the hospital that day is that I recently asked the people most likely to have accompanied me. Apparently Nicky brought me back to the flat, watched over me until I had eaten something and declared myself ready to sleep. Try as I might, I cannot remember anything of this. The following days are a mosaic of coloured pieces and clear glass, memories and absences.

These reactions – my mother's deflection, my erasure – shared key characteristics: they were involuntary and elemental, a retreat from the full realisation of our circumstances, that in delaying and reducing our engagement with grief made us appear more functional than we were, perhaps even a little detached.

There was a look I caught more than once in those early days – surprise, unease – when I behaved in ways that defied expectations of widowhood. It's not that I danced or sang or made tasteless jokes (though I'm sure I did make tasteless jokes). It was more that I was still recognisably myself. I had noticed this reaction to my widowed mother before I found myself on its receiving end.

So often the bereaved are judged as if there were a right way to do grief. The form that judgement takes is shaped by wider social attitudes. The irony is not lost on me that as the co-founder of the Women's Equality Party, it has taken my own widowhood to make me think about how this phenomenon plays out for women. Mourning rituals vary widely across time and cultures but there is a constant: women who survive their spouses are subject to tougher criticisms, customs and rules than other classes of bereaved. 'If I am to speak of womanly virtues to those of you who will henceforth be widows, let me sum them up in one short admonition,' said Pericles in his funeral oration for Athenian soldiers who had died in the opening skirmishes of the Peloponnesian War. 'To a woman not to show more weakness than is natural to her sex is a great glory, and not to be talked about for good or for evil among men.' Failure to wear widow's weeds – black clothing signalling their sad status – earned censure for Victorian widows. Queen Victoria drew criticism for the inverse behaviour, wearing widow's weeds for forty years after the death of Prince Albert, longer than the prissy era that bears her name deemed seemly.

Navigating popular ideas of widowhood can feel like being Goldilocks without the option of the third bowl of porridge. Whatever we choose risks being too hot or too cold. *We* risk being judged too hot or too cold. Our cultural heritage teems with steamy, rapacious, dangerous widows and their icy antitheses. Black Widow is both a *Marvel* assassin and the unrelated titular serial killer of a 1987 movie ('she mates and she kills'). *Jane Eyre*'s Mrs Reed stares mistily at a miniature of her dead husband but ignores his dying injunction to look after their niece, Jane, as if she were one of their own children. Instead she abuses her, then exiles her to the brutal Lowood School.

Underpinning these uneasy portrayals is a sense that widows, unlike other women, have power. The opposite remains true in swathes of the world where widows are routinely not only deprived of inheritances but treated *as* inheritance, to be passed on and enslaved. It was coverture, established in English common law in the twelfth century, that by omission granted to spinsters and widows rights not available to their wedded sisters. Under this convention, a married couple became, in economic terms, a single unit. That union saw possessions and other rights passed from bride to groom, making her by extension his chattel. Spinsters, by contrast, retained economic control and widows regained it, even if as women their rights were curtailed in many other respects.

*

My mother and I, in our deceptive calm, inadvertently tapped into deep-rooted folk memories and prejudices, though Pericles would surely have approved for all the wrong reasons. None of the people urging us to cry more or organise less did so from a position of anything but love. Others, equally benign in their intent, pushed premature life plans at us. Within days of our husbands dying, friends and family had told us we should move from our respective homes or at least avoid staying in them until we had regained strength. Different people react differently to loss, but both of us drew comfort precisely from the reminders we were warned against. We still do. The presence of our dearest departeds is something neither of us wishes to escape.

In truth we were neither strong nor weak, powerful nor fragile. We became all of those things and still are. My mother surprised herself in finding resilience she didn't know she possessed and coping with tasks and responsibilities she had for years left to John. Nor did she, in those first weeks, show signs of echoing Queen Victoria and withdrawing from the fray, though grief, lockdown and its closure of public toilets diminished her desire to venture far from home. John died on 22 December. On Christmas Day, she arrived at Andy's and my flat for the family meal I was cooking in John's stead. She wore a grey, cable-knit dress, patterned tights and ankle boots, with a sparkling of jewellery and her signature lipstick. She looked, acted and interacted almost as if nothing untoward had happened. Later she would ask me if Andy was all right. She noticed that he picked at his food.

She always notices things, and she has a ridiculously good memory, useful for the purposes of this book. I too used reliably to remember certain things – lists, dates, phone numbers – and accretions of detail that didn't, at the time, seem to matter.

Andy mentioned this facility in an interview with the *Sunday Times*, published two weeks after he died. The journalist Helen Cullen, who spoke to both of us separately for the newspaper's 'Relative Values' series, later sent me the recording of Andy. So strange and moving it was, hearing him from beyond the grave. He recounted an incident back in the early Nineties at the Blueprint Café near Tower Bridge. 'We went out one evening to a restaurant and the waiter happened to recognise me from Gang of Four, so he was quite chatty and then he said, "What's your order, madam? Do you want me to bring the menu back?" Catherine said, "No, I can remember it." "What, all of it?" "Yes, all of it," and he replied, "I'll give you a bottle of champagne if you can remember the whole menu." So she just recited the whole lot, including what came with everything, like twenty dishes. I knew she could do it, but he was very surprised and produced a bottle of champagne.'

Listening to this recording, I yearned to interrupt Andy, to add a missing element of exposition: the waiter offered to bring the menu back because the dish I'd ordered had run out. And, by the way, his name was Simon. That's how long-term couples often communicate, speaking across each other, issuing small additions and clarifications to their joint narrative. My mother and John were like that too. If you didn't know how much they loved each other, you might have thought they were bickering. 'Oh Anne,' John would say, rolling his eyes. 'Which of us is telling this story?'

A sadness in writing this book has been the absence of that affectionate, jousting dialogue, though my mother and I fall into similar habits when we meet in her living room. Are you sure that's right, we ask each other? Didn't that event precede this one? In search of answers, I pore over old text messages and WhatsApps, emails and my online diary. There are other resources too, including Andy's mobile and computer, but I'm inexplicably reluctant to switch them on and startled by the volume of correspondence when I do. Friends and strangers still send him messages to tell him how much he meant to them. Until his number was disconnected, there were voicemails. 'Andy, I miss you. I wish I had seen you more often. You've shaped my life more than you'll ever know.'

Needs must. I force myself to fire up his computer, look through the calendar on his phone. If only he and John could give you their version of events – and correct my mother's and mine. In the *Sunday Times* recording, Andy identifies me as an unreliable narrator. 'Memory's a funny thing, isn't it,' he says. 'I actually think she gets things wrong when she's looking back at certain events and I'm going "no that's not quite how it happened."'

My mother and I from the outset resolved in telling our stories to stick to the truth as closely as we could, even where it is painful or uncomfortable. My amnesia complicates the process and distresses me for other reasons too. Days have disappeared, but these were anyway disposable, post-Andy days. It is the sense of our life together slipping out of reach that torments me, his scent (I keep an unwashed t-shirt in a Ziploc bag, but it smells more of hospital than Andy), his stories. I drive myself mad, or madder, trying to remember his stories. There's one he used to tell about his youth involving a mix-up between Tony, a hash-dealing acquaintance, and the dealer's father, an upstanding, pillar-of-the-community also called Tony. The anecdote always made me laugh. Now I retrieve only fragments: Tony Senior answering the phone to a client of Tony Junior, who requests 'a pony' (£25's-worth) of Junior's wares;

a punchline ending with the Lady Bracknellesque exclamation 'a gymkhana?!' Was this tale inherently funny or did the humour, as so often the case, rely on Andy's delivery?

I remember the name of a waiter from three decades ago. How is it that other small details elude me? These turn out to matter at least as much as the big stuff. Yes, yes, so Andy was an extraordinary guitarist, a ground-breaking musician, something of a genius. Right now, my dearest wish is to find him in the studio, disturb him even if he's writing another trailblazing work, make him tell me, one last time, the story of Tony's dad.

That last Christmas dinner, he told no stories. He was quiet, abstracted. My attention was on my mother. My sisters and I had already begun to discuss with her what practical support we could offer. Catherine A would work with Cassie on the estate and with me on organising the funeral; Lise would handle the wake. On 27 December, I paid a visit to A. France & Son, the funeral director in Lamb's Conduit Street that three years earlier had handled the ceremony for Sara B, under instruction from me and her children. On 6 February, I would return to A. France for a third time to ask them to organise a cremation for Andy. I should have requested a bulk discount.

Death is monstrous. Sometimes it is funny in a monstrous kind of way. The fates that conspired to snatch John and Andy, then impose a nationwide lockdown amid a global pandemic, were having a right old laugh.

Chapter 2: Denial

'*I always knew I would lose you, but I never told you of my fears; of the night, six months into our relationship, when you curled up to me, your skin so smooth. When I reached for the light, I spotted a lesion on the nape of your neck, black as the future, obviously a melanoma. I loved you too much to deprive you of a last untroubled sleep, so said nothing, hit the switch and lay awake beside you for hours, dreading the dawn and what lay beyond that dawn. Such a strange thing: I wasn't neurotic. You can testify to that. I took risks with my own life. I still do. Yours seemed more fragile, even then. Of course, when I looked again, at first light, I could see that the mark was not a mole, but a piece of wax paper, the corner of a Mars wrapper. You always did like to eat chocolate in bed.*'

I wrote these words in August 2019, part of a novel that now will never be published and probably never deserved to be. In my reimagining of H. G. Wells' *The Time Machine*, the Time Traveller – a Silicon Valley tycoon – tricks the Narrator into accompanying him to a future shaped by a global pandemic. The Time Traveller deploys his technology in a self-aggrandising mission to tackle problems created by technology. The Narrator sees another possibility: she might bend time to save her partner of many years, who is dying.

When I embarked on the novel, months ahead of the first reports of an outbreak in Wuhan, the pandemic and its impact were fiction, my descriptions of the melanoma-that-wasn't and the partner who ate chocolate in bed, autobiography. The Narrator spoke in my voice and of my deepest terrors.

I suppose that in articulating these terrors, I hoped to stop them from materialising. Yet something else also compelled me to write – the absence of any other outlet. Andy was my closest companion. Our working lives could be demanding, but we always made time to talk. We wrote in adjacent rooms, cooked together, ate together, spent evenings lounging together, with friends or just the two of us. We agreed to leave serious discussions for daylight hours and our weekend walks. As we strolled, nothing was off bounds – nothing except the most serious topic of all. He would always shut down conversations that reminded him we couldn't live, as we were, forever.

'Rock musicians have shorter lives than other people.' This is the bald observation of an academic paper published in the scientific journal *Advances in Gerontology* and based on comparing the average age of death of nearly fifty thousand members of the creative professions.

Until the last two years of Andy's life, he seemed pretty healthy for a rock musician whose tours were more notable for their gourmet riders than for abstinence. Other bands argued with promoters about smoke machines and lasers; Andy pushed for good food and fine white wines, properly chilled. I remember his exasperation when Glastonbury, on a hot summer's day, ran out of ice.

At home, by mutual agreement and his personal choice, he lived more moderately, eating well and exercising daily. In his twenties, he underwent an emergency operation to excise a cancerous tumour and, because this was lawsuit-happy America, a string of lymph nodes. The experience left him with a scar from groin to sternum and clips holding him together that could be felt below the skin years later. It may also have underpinned his aversion to end-of-life discussions and his surprising lack of arrogance. Performers can be brittle and needy; he was neither, though he often did tell me, in jest, how lucky I was to be with him and that he was a genius. I would laugh, but both statements were true. We were always lucky, something I felt moved to acknowledge in a statement on the day he died: 'This pain is the price of extraordinary joy, almost three decades with the best man in the world.'

We met in 1991 at a 'page forty-six party'. Invitations, in those analogue days, had been extended to people living in the part of Islington mapped out on that page of the *London A–Z*. Neither of us did.

Our paths crossed by stroke of luck and our good fortune manifested itself in other ways too. No matter that we had marched against her: we belonged to the minority of the population that had thrived during Margaret Thatcher's premiership. The venue, a warehouse flat with a suspended pool replacing one wall to create a human aquarium, spoke to the affluence of our intersecting social circles, musicians and writers, artists and actors.

Wealth cannot shield you from death. I think, now, of friends at that party. Our hosts were Richard Paxton and Heidi Locher, architects of the flat and of other buildings including Soho Theatre. Richard died suddenly at 49; so too one of their guests, the author Douglas Adams. The barrister, Jane Belson, later

Douglas's wife, was also there that night. She would outlive him by a mere decade.

Yet money certainly gives you better odds of living longer. A life expectancy gap of nearly a decade for men and two-thirds' that period for women separates the UK's wealthiest from the poorest. The income gap plays out in bereavement too, in the scrabble to meet the exorbitant costs of death, financial and emotional.

Such thoughts had never troubled my life as I wandered through Rick and Heidi's flat and laughed at an unfeasibly handsome man who stood next to the buffet, a serving bowl under his arm, scooping out trifle with his hand. Andy hadn't been able to find a plate or cutlery. We started talking and eventually ended up on the terrace, where he serenaded me with The Drifters' song, 'Up on the Roof'. 'And if this old world starts getting you down,' he sang, 'there's room enough for two.'

We met again the following weekend and never looked back – or much into the future. We were busy and happy. Then, nine years later, a cold wind blew through our Eden. Andy's university friend Yannis didn't mean to fall from the flat roof of his apartment block; drunk and arguing with a lover, he lost his footing. The singer Michael Hutchence hadn't planned to die either, succumbing to a suicidal impulse after a sleepless night and a turbulent few years. Andy and he had been working on an album together; we were godparents to his daughter with Paula Yates. His death left Paula, who was both a cause of the turbulence and Michael's sanctuary from it, with a double burden of loss and guilt, and ensnared in a skein of administrative wrangles. After one of many rescue missions to her house, summoned by some terrible crisis or her intractable sorrow, I returned home to find Andy in the kitchen, doing the washing up. 'Do you think we should get married?' he asked. I supposed so. We had seen in Paula's struggles that love counted for little in the eyes of the law or the rapacious music industry. She attended our wedding in September 1999. A year later, our friend Jo found her cold and final in her bed, the victim of an accidental overdose.

Michael's death had plunged Andy into despair and me into coping mode. I tended to him, to Paula, to her daughters. Paula's death took my breath away – at least half an hour I gasped for air when we woke to the headlines. Then it propelled me into a spiral of activity that I couldn't, at the time, name. All I knew was that I had never been more productive. I seemed to require neither food nor sleep and often took long walks at night. Scared of further and greater loss, I recoiled from the person I most feared losing, the only person who could comfort me, deluding myself that I needed neither him nor comfort.

Hello grief. So cruel you can be, tearing apart families, setting lovers against each other, urging people in the teeth of involuntary life changes to make more and faster change. Andy and I were lucky, again. After a difficult time, we found our way back, held each other tighter. Others are less fortunate. Grief poisoned my mother's relationship with her own mother, Ruth. How could she, a child already reeling from the death of her father, cope with the loss of her little brother, much less understand Ruth's anguish? My mother felt – still feels – that given a choice between her children, my grandmother would have preserved Kenny's life, directing the lightning bolt at her eldest instead.

These days grief is my familiar, a shadow I know as well as myself; that is to say, not quite as well as I think. Some days its shape-shifting ways still surprise me, a bruise that inflicts bruises. My spatial awareness is shot. Yesterday I walked into a table. This morning, I took a break from writing this chapter and in the kitchen, beneath a new portrait of Andy created in tribute to him by the street artist Shepard Fairey, danced, sobbing, to 'Up on the Roof'. Another day grief might sit on my chest, immobilising me in an echo of Andy, on his last day at home, laid out and struggling for breath. It isn't an easy companion, is no substitute for the companionship it replaces. Yet it is more than the price of love. It is love. We, the bereaved, must learn not just to live with it, but to make it welcome.

At 56, Andy was diagnosed with sarcoidosis, an inflammatory disease that can affect any part of the body but in his case targeted the lungs. Initially he mistook his minor breathlessness for a return of the asthma that had troubled him since child-hood. He consulted a specialist, George Santis, Professor of Thoracic Medicine and Interventional Bronchoscopy at King's College Hospital and a consultant physician for Guy's and St Thomas's, who prescribed a course of steroids that quickly sorted him out. Recurrences were mild. Then came a bout that hit him harder and responded more slowly to treatment. The steroids, in higher doses, eventually did their stuff, but at a cost. He couldn't sleep, using the fevered nights to write a new album, developing diabetes as a side-effect of the drug and losing lung capacity to scarring. Professor Santis regularly checked on his progress.

That February, I joined Andy at the start of a Gang of Four tour that would cross the US from the west coast to the mid-winter east, culminating in New York. Our arrival coincided with a polar vortex that turned most of the US into a snow globe and unleashed on California sleeting rain. Water dripped from the skylight of the tour bus, pooling on the floor. Already

Andy seemed too weak for the slog ahead, endless days on the road, the load-ins and soundchecks, the interviews, the kinetic performances, the backstage revelries abbreviated only once the load-out was completed and the bus set off again. The gigs, though, were brilliant and he was in his element. At The Roxy in Los Angeles, flanked by Shepard Fairey and the musician Tom Morello. I watched Andy smash a guitar and make magnificent noise.

After I flew home, his health declined. In Denver, the altitude, in combination with his reduced lung function, sent him to hospital. He managed to play that night. As the band traversed America, he got sicker, blaming the cold air. By the time they reached Woodstock, he had lost feeling in his legs and had to be carried on to the stage. The next day, his bandmates rebelled, refusing to perform unless he obtained medical assurance that he was fit to do so. He called me from a New York hospital, pleading with me to persuade them to change their minds. Instead I backed them and, after his return to England, urged him to seek medical attention. Our GP took one look at him and sent him straight to hospital. He was there for a few days, then discharged himself. He had work to do.

In retrospect, it's obvious that I wasn't alone in my intimations of his mortality. Andy's nominal reason for concealing his illness was that promoters would stop booking him if they thought him a bad bet. When I study photos of him from that time, I see fear in his eyes. He did his best to maintain focus on the present – *Live In the Moment*, as he punningly titled a recent live album – and to trust in a future mapped out in tour dates and deadlines. 'The doctors will just tell me to take more steroids,' he argued, or 'All it needs is a bit of warm weather and I'll be fine.'

When spring arrived, he appeared to be right. We attended

a wedding in Hastings in May, a second wedding in the town in July, enjoyed walks along the clifftops. That summer, staying with friends in Spain, I took a photograph of Andy against a fresco in the former monastery of Santes Creus, a skull above his head. In September, in Athens, we celebrated our twentieth wedding anniversary and twenty-ninth year together. The next day we wandered contentedly around the archaeological museum, surrounded by reminders of human transience. Gang of Four played in the city that night. It was the last great performance of theirs I would see, the last anniversary Andy and I would spend together. In my bones I knew what was coming. So why did I not try harder to talk to him about it?

Fear of death is rational. Our responses to that fear more rarely are. We try to outrun mortality, to shield ourselves from the clear, sharp pain of loss. Let me share with you, from a place of pain and in the story of Andy's death, a lesser ambition: to remove not the pain, but the avoidable stress and distress that too often cloud it.

In the years we were together, Andy and I built and made and created things that required effort and dedication: music, books, campaigns and organisations, and a flat above a recording studio in a space without planning permissions for either. We obtained those permissions and navigated any number of more complex challenges that confronted us during our working lives, including legal skirmishes and lawsuits. We knew our way around forms and institutions. We were well prepared for anything life threw at us – except death. Andy died before making a Will or sharing his last wishes or passwords or the secret of how to fix the television when it goes on the blink.

In a later chapter I touch on the difference planning for

the end of life can make for the dying and those they leave. First I must deal with something far more uncomfortable. Did Andy and I, in trying to ignore his fate, advance it? What if instead of collusive silence, I'd offered him a way to admit to and address our mutual fears? Imagine if we'd known how to talk about death as easily as we debated politics or the books we were reading or, a question that preoccupied us, what to have for dinner.

It wasn't until November, nine months after his hospitalisation and apparent recovery, that I realised quite how tightly braced I was against a relapse. My sisters and I had plotted with our stepmother to arrange a surprise visit to my father on his ninety-first birthday. As we sat in his house in Manchester, a WhatsApp came through from Gang of Four's tour manager, a photo of the band accepting the applause of the crowd with the simple caption, all in capital letters: 'WE DID IT!' I surprised everyone, including myself, by bursting into tears.

The day before, I had messaged the tour manager, concerned that Andy sounded breathless on the phone. 'Beijing is very cold!' the tour manager replied. 'We are all a bit short of breath.' Now the tour was over, in grand style, a catalogue of full houses and five-star reviews, and my love was coming home.

We'd developed a trick over the years, Andy and I. Instead of reuniting in our flat at the end of his tours, we would book ourselves into a hotel, allowing twenty-four hours to catch up on neutral territory before he crashed back into a space that in his absence was always tidy and quiet. It is tidy and quiet now.

On this occasion, I broke with tradition. I just wanted him back. He looked tired but his lungs didn't sound too bad, an observation confirmed by his thoracic specialist, Professor Santis, the following week. The day he imparted this encouraging news, my mother took the call from my stepfather to tell her that he wouldn't be coming home from UCLH for the time being. We commiserated with her and agreed to join her two nights later for a muted celebration of her birthday at a restaurant booked for the occasion by John.

The following days and weeks will be pocked with hollow celebrations, Christmas parties, birthdays, feeble hope vainly flapping its tinsel wing. We visit John in hospital. When my mother is in earshot, he talks of a fictional future. After he dies, the festivities continue. Andy and I bring in the new year with family and friends in Italy. At midnight, someone hands out sparklers. I watch his burn down and cannot stand the symbolism. By this stage it is no longer possible to pretend that he is even remotely OK. If I'd realised how sick he was, I'd never have agreed to travel to this undulating countryside, where paths we used to walk taunt him with their cambers and gradients. On our return to Gatwick, he can no longer manage its flat expanses either. I find a wheelchair and somehow manoeuvre him, our twin cases and computer bags to the train station. I'm lucky, I think, to be strong, just like my mother, who until so recently had wheeled John about the place. I will be Andy's carer, as she was John's. Already I am shedding work commitments, rearranging my life to the service of his.

Three years, my mother looked after John. I tell myself I will have longer to tend to Andy. He was born amid a hubbub of new year fireworks. In Italy, at the moment his sparkler splutters its last, he has turned just 64, hardly any age at all.

He and I support each other in our denial. Our fantasies are not the same, though Andy is beginning to acknowledge the possibility that he may have to make some changes. He keeps booking tour dates and working on music, but he also starts looking at property in warmer climates, still trying to convince himself and me that cold air is the culprit. I imagine living in such a place, tranquil and content, enabling Andy to write music. I know that he shouldn't tour again and wonder what it will take to make him accept this too.

At night, pipe dreams give way to living nightmares. Andy's specialist has given him a small, portable oxygen supply for the last tour. He didn't need it on the road; now he depends on it. We sleep to the hiss and pop of its pump.

He takes higher doses of steroids and an immunosuppressant, Methotrexate, to try to dampen what we assume to be a particularly acute episode of sarcoidosis. Despite the steroids, he remains lethargic, dozing through the days and barely moving from our bedroom. When I persuade him to see our GP, she tells him he should be in hospital. He refuses. I discover after Andy's death that he ignored the same recommendation from Professor Santis. Andy insists that hospitalisation will make him worse. He wants to be at home.

Much later – too late – I will ask questions that I should have pursued, without let-up and to their logical conclusion, no matter how much Andy and I would have hated the answers. The reply I receive from Professor Santis, in its caution and kindness, tells me what I needed to know: that there is a chance, however slight, that the outcome could have been happier if we had acted sooner. 'It is difficult to know if Andy's touring contributed to his deterioration,' he writes. 'I suspect not... I doubt again if an earlier admission would have made much difference. Unfortunately, it is impossible to answer with any certainty.'

On 18 January, I find Andy slumped in a chair, conscious

but colourless. Finally I tell him I am calling an ambulance and even then we bargain. First he must have a bath. Then he asks for a glass of Puligny-Montrachet. I refuse and will always upbraid myself for that pointless rigidity. The paramedic suspects sepsis and summons a blue-light ambulance to take us to St Thomas's hospital.

Even then we delay its departure. Andy wants his computer with him, external hard drives, address book. He's planning already to work from his hospital bed. This, too, he will do, right until the moment he is forced to stop. He will cease building a fictive future only when he can no longer breathe.

Chapter 3: Death

28/01/20 Day shift

Hey Andrew,

My name is Amy and I'm the nurse that has looked after you today.

This morning when we met, you had been struggling with your breathing, so you had agreed for the doctors to put you to sleep and put a breathing tube in your mouth to help you with your oxygenation and carbon dioxide.

Also today you have had lines inserted into your neck and groin to allow us to give you important medications to help your blood pressure and antibiotics for your lungs.

In the evening I attached you to a dialysis machine which is kinda like an outside kidney. It's going to help clear potassium from your body, which has been rather high today. It makes lots of noises almost like a Gameboy sound. Other machines have been beeping today almost like a song without lyrics ☺. You have had lots of close friends visit you and Catherine has been here by your side all day.

Keep working hard. It's been a pleasure looking after you.
Best wishes
Amy ☺

29/01/20

HI ANDY, WAKE UP.
GOT SOMETHING I NEED TO ASK YOU.
C YA TOMORROW GILL-IAN.
THOMAS

There are thirty-six entries in Andy's critical care diary, written by the nurses looking after him and the friends and family who came to see him. The diaries are allocated to patients in comas, their visitors encouraged to leave messages. This can assist with recovery, a nurse explained. Patients brought round after protracted periods of medically induced oblivion may be confused and anxious. The diaries help them to reconstruct the missing days and weeks.

Andy's diary performs a different function. It is a testament of love, an assertion of the person he will always be. Too often, lives are defined by their endings. We remember the failing body, the diminished cognitive abilities. The people who love Andy refuse to do this. A line on the screen behind his bed charts the electrical activity of his original mind. We are warned that it would be cruel to rouse him to awareness of the tubes and catheters. We should not even touch him, lest this prompts his brain to spark, though his brother Martin and I are given special dispensation to hold his hands.

The diary becomes a manifesto for life. One by one, the visitors add to it wonderful, tiny fragments of Andy. Inevitably, many of the entries focus on Andy's passionate pursuit of pleasure, stories of food and drink and riotous company. 'You live two years for every one I do,' observes one friend. 'I won't tell anyone what happened between you and that monkey,' says another.

Our brother-in-law, Catherine A's husband Keith, writes of an occasion at a starchy club, a significant birthday or a wake. 'You had your top button undone and your tie was loosely hanging. "They're never going to throw me out," you said. "My tie is from Eton."' The tie was indeed from Eton. Andy no Old Etonian he, always enjoyed testing the boundaries and reflexes of the establishment.

The individual entries are vivid, but the composite picture is more striking still. Andy has connected with so many people so deeply. Young men fight their way through a dense undergrowth of reticence and social programming to pour out their hearts. He has been the first adult whose company they actively sought out, whose friendship they cherish. Soon he will be another first for them, too: the first to ruffle their assumption that death is for the old and spent.

Most of Andy's visitors have not seen him in the intermediate stage between admission to the ICU and this, his penultimate state. He wanted to keep his illness quiet, clung to his plans to finish some of his own music and a covers album he'd been working on for two years, famous bands and musicians recording Gang of Four tracks. During his first ten days in hospital, he pushed forward with these projects, accepting visits only from people directly involved in this work and from a small clutch of immediate family and close friends.

At first, I went along with his desire for secrecy. The doctors sounded optimistic. He was, they told us, the healthiest person in ICU. Soon they would transfer him to a high-dependency unit, thence to a general ward and home. Later, they began to warn me of a more difficult scenario, a long hospital incarceration, weeks if not months. I could easily imagine what this might entail. The adjacent beds, each encircled by their own plangent orchestras of monitors and machines, held veterans, one already on the ward for more than a hundred days and not expected to leave any time soon. The weeks had whittled away at visitor numbers until only spouses or close relatives remained, drifting from bedsides to the family room and back, and launching occasional expeditions to the outer edges of this limbo, a food court near the main entrance. Purgatory, it turns out, looks and smells like a motorway services.

One night, when Andy could still speak but was tired beyond speech by the effort of breathing, the nurses urged me to go home. I was reluctant to do so, though my back had moulded itself to the curve of the plastic chair. What if he needed me and I wasn't there? He seemed increasingly disoriented. 'Let's hope we beat the Germans,' says a departing friend, referring to the forthcoming match they have just discussed, pitting Andy's beloved Manchester United against a German side. 'I predict Russia will enter the war soon,' Andy replies. The films he watched as a boy have never left him. Throughout our life together, he dreams of the trenches and of bombing raids, waking me with strangled cries. Did he fight to the last, I now wonder; replay in his drugged final hours *The Dam Busters* or *633 Squadron* with its pithy soundbites? 'I'm against death, but it happens anyway.'

The nurses are firm. I must rest. The hours I am spending in the hospital cannot be sustained for the long haul ahead. Andy is stable. Nothing will change before morning.

It is late, but I decide to walk home. If Andy continues on this level trajectory or begins to show improvement, I plan to fulfil the only external commitment I have not yet cancelled. The Globe Theatre has commissioned me to write and perform a piece about Paula Yates. I accept the challenge, meaning to reset public perceptions of her, to attest to wit, humour and achievement erased in the media telling of her story. As I write, I find that I am swimming in grief. Learning my lines seems less daunting than getting through the performance without crying. Almost twenty years this sorrow has crouched, ready to spring. My route from St Thomas's takes me past the London Eye, along the south bank of the Thames. I recite the play, as I go, remember all the words, crumple just once, at a mention of Andy.

Returning to the hospital next morning, I recite my lines again, wearing headphones to make it look as if I'm speaking on my mobile. Grief has not yet stolen every fuck I have to give. At the base of the London Eye, the phone rings. I recognise the number: the ICU. A nurse, a different one, tells me that Andy has just been placed in a coma.

I don't fully understand the sentence but cannot escape its import. A doctor has already explained that putting Andy on a ventilator would be a last resort. Patients with damaged lungs tend to have poor outcomes with mechanical breathing. Sarcoidosis is not, we've learned, the primary cause of his hospitalisation. Pneumocystis jiroveci pneumonia, an opportunistic infection, has settled in lungs striated by past inflammations. Healthy lungs appear dark on scans. Andy's are white as bone.

Before the nurse finishes speaking, I am running. There is a long, signposted route through the hospital to the East Wing, past the Clinical Decision Unit and Resuscitation, where Andy spent his first night, then a switchback and another stretch of corridor to reach the lifts. Ten days in, I know a shortcut through the North Wing. As I run, I nearly crash into Ed Miliband, a work acquaintance, startle him by blurting out something about Andy and comas, set off running again.

Why do I run? However fast I move, the destination will be the same.

Things done or undone, things said or unsaid: some percentage of grief is always contaminated by regret. Well-meaning people will try to reason your regrets away, but this is neither possible nor, I suspect, desirable. I don't know for certain, but I think my grief for Paula floored me after nineteen years because I hadn't looked it in the eye, acknowledged its constituent parts and causes. Grief, like life and the living, breathing relationships death curtails, is triumphantly messy, full of ambiguities and what-ifs.

I do know that I will always be sorry for these things – that I didn't break through Andy's resistance to talking about death, that I didn't get him to hospital sooner, that I didn't bring him wine before the ambulance arrived, that I wasn't there that morning when they put him to sleep. I would have urged him to keep trying to breathe on his own, warned him of the mortality statistics for people in his situation. I would have told him that I love him.

Might such an intervention have changed his mind and, if so, what then? Another day or two of suffering, followed by the same outcome? Or salvation? Parallel universes are thought experiments, nothing more nor less. They provide no definitive answers; but they can help to define the questions that attend every death.

Recently a new and thorny question keeps snagging my attention. The news is full of reports of miracle recoveries from Covid-19. The former children's laureate Michael Rosen, ten years Andy's senior, survived seven weeks on a ventilator and is now at home. Another survivor, a man called Mal Martin, endured sixty-one days on a ventilator. His wife, Sue, told the BBC that doctors declared 'he was at the brink and there was nothing further they could do for him. The chance of his surviving... was almost zero.'

Inevitably I ask myself this: did I agree too easily to switching off Andy's machines? When the critical care consultant, another Andy, warned me that, barring an overnight rally by his namesake, we would be having a difficult conversation the following day, I understood exactly what he meant. My sister Lise, standing with me and hearing the same words, perceived a sliver of hope. Perhaps in my determination to keep my emotions subordinate to reason, I overlooked those slivers.

I remembered the long-running legal case involving a young American woman, Terry Schiavo, kept on life support not Michael Rosen's seven weeks but a full seven years as her parents challenged the decision of her husband and doctors to remove her feeding tube. Her parents' stance seemed to me selfish at the time, but then again, mine may have been equally so. I acted according to a fixed idea of the right thing to do rather than listening to my sister or my own heart.

Andy's organs were failing. He was judged too weak to tolerate an ECMO machine to oxygenate his blood outside of the body. It was anyway hard to imagine where they would find room for it. By now he resembled a dog walker in a London park, tethered to entities of different shapes and sizes by leashes of his own essence. It had become increasingly difficult to negotiate the equipment to exercise my small dispensation, to hold his hand.

And so I sat down with the consultant and agreed the date for my love to die: 1 February. This would give enough time for those who wanted to see him to travel to London, not least his band: John, the singer, with his wife Laura, from Hastings; Thomas, the bass player, from Glasgow; Tobias, the drummer, from Berlin. There had been changing line-ups over the years. Andy was Gang of Four's only consistent presence. The dynamics of this harmonious incarnation resembled a family unit, Andy, perhaps more mischievous uncle than father figure, the younger musicians bonded to him much as his real-life nephew Isaac had always been, by deep love and a sense that Andy opened the world to new experiences and possibilities.

Once the date was set, the band and my sisters organised shifts. The ICU permitted us to keep watch throughout the nights. I couldn't bear the idea of him being alone. I managed the steady stream of visitors, two-by-two at the bedside, the maximum allowed, to say goodbye. They arrived with tales of candlelit vigils for the EU and Brexiteers surging through the streets. It all seemed very remote, a distant planet where political decisions determined personal outcomes. Only recently, Andy had worried about Brexit interrupting his supplies of life-sustaining medicine. Now disposing of his medicine would be one of the first small tasks of sadmin and the UK's rupture with Europe a surreal backdrop to something more irrevocable still, more momentous by far.

At some point, the band and I commandeer the family room.

We are joined by Andy's former manager Aaron and others associated with Gang of Four's long history. We are grappling with the realisation that they will have to put out a statement after he dies. John quickly drafts something. He doesn't need to reach deep to know what he wants to say:

This is so hard for us to write, but our great friend and Supreme Leader has died today.

Andy's final tour in November was the only way he was ever really going to bow out; with a Stratocaster around his neck, screaming with feedback and deafening the front row.

His uncompromising artistic vision and commitment to the cause meant that he was still listening to mixes for the upcoming record, whilst planning the next tour from his hospital bed.

But to us, he was our friend – and we'll remember him for kindness and generosity, his fearsome intelligence, bad jokes, mad stories and endless cups of Darjeeling tea. He just so happened to be a bit of a genius too.

One of the best ever to do it, his influence on guitar music and the creative process was inspiring for us, as well as everyone who worked alongside him and listened to his music. And his albums and production work speak for themselves. Go give 'em a spin for him…

Love you, mate.
John, Thomas and Tobias
GANG OF FOUR

*

Andy died, as he lived, to a soundtrack that meant something.
I chose Fauré's Requiem. We had often fallen asleep to its
strains.

There are other decisions too. The level of care in the ICU
is astonishing. Coronavirus has yet to deplete its resources or
crowd patients into every available nook. We change protective
plastic aprons many times a day, as if these items will never run
out; I have been at his bedside since his admission, but for the
day of John's funeral. In one of our final pieces of luck, Andy's
final illness narrowly precedes the declaration of the pandemic
and the accompanying strictures that would have kept me at
an agonising distance from him.

His ICU bed occupies a space intended for two, at one end
of the ward, at a remove from other patients. The hospital
understands that we are an extended family unit, blood relatives
and friends and band, and will allow many more of us than
usual to be present for his death.

The nurse offers to prepare him. Gently she washes his hair,
oh so carefully she shaves him. Nothing must wake him, but
his is not a chin that willingly yields to razors. It is both square
and curved, a handsome chin with a Kirk Douglas dimple that
we call by Andy's maternal name, Dalrymple. It's tricky to
shave a Dalrymple.

Somehow the nurse manages but then there is another hitch.
A small section of his upper lip is covered by the mouthpiece
of the ventilator. He cannot die with a Hitler moustache, I say.
She finds a colleague who holds the plastic out of the way
while she works.

For Cassie, Maurice's death is too raw and recent for her
to contemplate the extinction of the brother-in-law she also
adores. Silently she leaves. Martin and I flank the bed. Lise,

Isaac, the band and tour manager, Nicky and Aaron take up positions behind me. I recall the Sun King and his *levée*, the Versailles ceremony in which courtiers observed and applauded the rising of the sovereign. A newspaper on the window sill carries a Brexit headline: 'The Day We Said Goodbye'. This is the day we attend my king's *couchée*.

The consultant stands at the end of the bed. The nurses have already unhooked the noisy dialysis machine and most of the other hardware. Now they remove Andy's breathing tube.

Minute one: I stroke his beautiful face.

Minute two: The colour ebbs, as if the tips of my fingers applied a gloss of ivory.

Minute three: His eyelids aren't quite shut. I see the green of his irises, the beautiful green.

Minute four: I check the monitor for spikes in his brain activity. He must not feel or fear.

Minute five: How many times have I told him in the past minutes that I love him? This is the only thing left to say but I will never be able to say it enough.

Minutes six and seven: I kiss him, his forehead, his nose, his Dalrymple.

Minute eight: On the other side of the bed, Martin shakes with stifled sobs.

Minute nine: He is so pale now, my love, so pale.

Minute ten: I squeeze his hand and sense a difference.

Minute eleven: Surely, I say to the consultant, it is over. He shakes his head.

Minute twelve: The consultant speaks, pronounces Andy dead. I cannot let go his hand or turn around, even when the sound starts behind me, tentative at first and then more confident, applause. The king is dead. Long live the king.

How lightly we use phrases about love. I'm sure I must have told Andy over the years that I love him more than life itself. In this moment, I know that this is both true and impossible. Love is life, not external to it. It takes on a new form after death. We call it grief.

Instagram post by Isaac, 2 February 2020. The photo shows Andy and me holding baby Isaac (these days he is a tall, self-contained 19-year-old). Andy is handing him a beer.

Andy, where do I even start?

Thank you. Thank you for being so much more than just my uncle. Thank you for teaching me everything my parents didn't want me to know about. Thank you for showing me how to be a wine connoisseur, age 6. Thank you for handing me my first ever guitar and then teaching me how to keep my entire street up at night playing it. Thank you for talking to me about Manchester United whenever I was bored at dinner. Thank you for your crazy stories, your questionable advice, your weird games and most importantly the amount of time you invested into looking like an idiot just to make me laugh.

Yesterday I truly lost not only an uncle, but also a role model. So much of who I am today was shaped by you and it pains me not only to have lost you so soon but also to know that future generations of our family will never have the chance to meet you. I miss you, I love you. Rest in Peace, Andy

The first letter to John

People often say of couples that they 'share a life together'. This isn't always a meaningful phrase. It's possible to share a home and little else of significance. Some partnerships are based on nothing more substantial than apathy, financial calculus or fear.

Imagine, by contrast, two people united, by passionate choice, for more than forty years, involved in each other's interests, seldom parted and in constant communication about big things and small. Then imagine the loss when that life is no longer shared.

You will understand why my mother, cut adrift from John only to be confronted in her grief with further, devastating loss, turned once more to him. You will understand why she began to write.

Here is the first of her letters.

27 March 2020

Dear John,

I can't believe it is over three months since we saw each other. I speak to you every day, but you are not there to reply. I hope you are well and comfortable where you are, no longer in pain and able to breathe and walk. And I hope you are missing me as much as I do you. I can hardly believe you loved me for all those years, and I adored you. One uses the term 'other half' lightly, but you were truly mine.

Quite a few things have happened since 22 December, none of them good, and I wanted to catch you up on them. Because you could not, after all, come home for Christmas, we had a Mayer family dinner at Catherine and Andy's. Delicious food, as they always produce, and a close family group. Christmas Day was bright and sunny, and I had a good walk in the morning before going to dinner mid-afternoon, so all in all not too miserable.

Boxing Day, on the other hand, was freezing, windy, and with torrential rain. Michael and Jeanine came to visit in the morning on their way to spend the day with their daughter and her family, and as I closed the door behind them at precisely 1 p.m. it hit me for the first time at full force that I was in this house ALONE, without you forever, and with no visitors to divert me for the foreseeable future. Catherine A and Keith had plans of their own and my tribe took off for Italy on the morning of the 27th and did not come back until after New Year. So I was really, really alone over the weekend which embraced our thirty-ninth wedding anniversary and New Year's Eve and New Year's Day. Your long hospital stays had prepared me for time alone in the house but with the prospect of talking to you frequently and visiting you at least once a day. This was entirely different. A kind of solitude I had never experienced and a terrible ache which was never going to stop.

At Christmas dinner I sat next to Andy, who was pale and quiet. He hardly touched his food and seemed uncharacteristically uncommunicative. Catherine rang me once or twice from Italy to say that she was worried about him and that over the New Year's weekend he had been tired, unwell, breathless and not very involved with the usual houseful gathered there at Lise and Angus's to celebrate NYE. The weather apparently was sunny and perfect for walks but Andy (and Catherine out of solidarity) did not go on any of the walks.

Sunday, 5 January found all the 'kids' at our house beginning to go through your papers. I am still adjusting to the fact that our five daughters are now four. When Sarah died three years ago, you could never quite bring yourself to talk about her and now you are both gone. You and Sarah were so very close and I know that her death in some way contributed to yours. I have lost many people but never a child, and I do not know how you bore it.

Back to 5 January; I am sure you remember those untidy stacks about which I never stopped moaning. You were not a messy person by nature and the accumulation of unsorted and unfiled papers bore witness to your increasing inability to master the stairs or the boring minutiae of daily life. Being honest, though, filing neatly and sensibly was never your outstanding accomplishment! We believed that the executors would be Cassie and Catherine A, and they started dividing things up in a very business-like way. My Catherine took on the job of planning your funeral and Lise the wake, for which Angus had generously said we could use his house. I neglected to say earlier that I had rung our solicitor Paul on the day after you died, and he had recommended a young colleague, Kimberley, to handle the probate. They would, he said, be back at work on 6 January, hence the timing of the workday at ours.

Their return to work found me faced with the unpalatable knowledge that we never signed those new Wills we worked so hard on in 2018. We had bulging envelopes with Power of Attorney but no Wills. Paul accepts some of the blame for this and my Will is now signed and waiting for my demise in my file. So I have had to use the Will you made in 1998, in which I am your Executor.

I won't spend pages complaining about the task. For someone like me who never properly grew up with respect to grappling with finances or technology or business matters (and I blame myself for this), it has been an unending nightmare. You knew what you were doing but it has been difficult to piece it all together and, of course, once the year began in earnest, the girls were all back at work with little time to spare. I am getting there slowly, with no thanks to a lot of those firms nor recompense for the hours I have spent trying to ring the bank and other organisations while listening to the worst canned music in the world. Anyway, probate is just a drop in the bucket compared to what was to come.

Your funeral was on 22 January and Andy was not there. Three days before it, he was rushed to St. Thomas's Hospital with severe breathing difficulties. He was diagnosed with pneumonia (sound familiar?) and put to bed much like you with oxygen but otherwise his usual persona. He had loads of visitors and everybody told Catherine the situation was manageable. The day after your funeral, on Catherine's birthday, I went to visit them both and he was chatty and alert although the staff were clearly concerned about his loss of appetite. Instead of getting better, he went downhill. They put him in an induced coma to try to give him time to recover, but his systems just caved in. Catherine and others kept all-night vigils and on Saturday, 1 February 2020, Andy died. There were just five weeks between your two deaths.

As you might expect, Catherine has been incredible. Andy was intestate, his affairs were more complex than yours and he has records due to appear. So for his young widow, it was a total car crash with people working on the music and paperwork all over as Andy was also messier than you, although not by much! And like me, she does her crying in private and keeps a resolute face to the world.

You might think this news terrible enough, but there is more, much more. Back in the autumn when no one in the Western world would have noticed, a man in the city of Wuhan came down with a virus which may have passed to him from a bat. The market in that city apparently sells all kinds of wildlife to customers, who happily consume them. Bats have had coronavirus for centuries but in 2019 for the very first time it appears to have leapt across the species and infected a human being. Within what seemed seconds, that city was in lockdown with thousands of illnesses and hundreds of deaths. But, hey, it was in central China, not even Beijing, and we all looked the other way.

As I write there is no nation in the entire world which is not affected by the disease. Thousands have already died, and hundreds of thousands are infected. After China the worst-hit nations are Italy, Spain and the United States, but the UK is catching up fast. And London is the hot spot. We are all under house arrest here, allowed to go out only for essential shopping and one walk a day. So instead of just being lonely and missing you, I am in isolation for weeks, perhaps months, and in fear for my life. And as all businesses are also closed, just getting hold of things requires strategies. This is where my lack of knowledge and fear of online has really hobbled me, far more than probate, as everybody is living online. But even that isn't easy as things like grocery deliveries are virtually impossible to arrange and panic buying has emptied the main supermarkets.

No end is in sight and we are told three months minimum. I write as I have completed only one week of that period. It is a horror story of such proportions that we will reach for words to describe it forever. Major conference centres are being turned into wartime hospitals with thousands of beds and woe betide if anything else is wrong with you. You and Andy would not, could not, have received the care you did or had your families around you. And you were both so vulnerable that we would have been constantly on our guard against coronavirus.

And lest you think this is all a poor me story – and it is partly, as I am imprisoned in the house and know from the news reports that, at my age, if I get very sick they will let me die – try to imagine the outside world. The only things that are open are supermarkets, pharmacies, newsagents. Nothing else is commercially alive. Oxford Street shuttered and shut. No pubs, bars, restaurants, theatres, opera houses, galleries or museums. Schools and universities are closed, and A levels and GCSEs are abandoned. Catherine A is teaching remotely from her home and your grandson Tom will have to be assessed in another way but cannot sit his exams. Isaac has a place at university but doubts it will even be open next September.

And a special word about sport, which you loved so much. I learned recently from a charming obituary written by your friend Stephen for your school newsletter that you broke every possible running record while still at Bishop Wordsworth's, as well as playing rugby. When we met you were a near-professional at hockey and together we played tennis until the year before you died and, as you will remember, walked miles in the

Yorkshire Dales when we lived in Leeds and climbed mountains in all sorts of countries.

People are forbidden to do team sports now or travel to beauty spots and spectator sports are off the menu too. We were into the rugby world championship when that got stopped, as did, after much confusion and to-ing and fro-ing, football, golf and tennis. There will be no Wimbledon nor Olympics this year. Cheltenham races went ahead but Aintree was cancelled.

Without sport or theatre reviews, the newspapers are so thin and anaemic one wonders how long they have got. Needless to say, my beloved Pilates seems a distant dream although it is not yet two whole weeks since I had a class.

We are in the midst of an apocalypse, like all those films which used to be so popular, when the protagonist returns to his native land years in the future and cannot recognise it. We cannot use public transport unless it is vital to the nation and even all the online services, which I cannot figure out anyway, are slowing down.

Both the US and UK are headed for serious recession. Trump keeps saying the US economy is more important than people's lives, but one-seventh of all the cases in the world are in New York City. Boris Johnson and several of the cabinet have the virus. Today we heard Prince Charles does too. There is literally no other news. A world empty of anything except coronavirus.

Easter looms and then what would have been your eighty-fourth birthday. All European nations have sealed their borders and there are no flights and no travel. All the airlines are pleading for help, but the government has splashed out so much to rescue people without work that they are getting very short shrift.

So this tough old Bird, pun intended, will spend Easter alone as she has spent every day since you died but, since last weekend, truly alone. For weeks and weeks stretching ahead. Who could have foreseen these disasters strung together like poisonous Christmas lights: you, then Andy, then the killer virus. Brexit is there too; we did leave on 31 January, but it is a mark of how strange and terrible things are that it has faded into temporary insignificance. Your almost new, smart, hybrid VW car still sits motionless, unused and unloved in the garage, your motorised scooter like a spare chair in the big room. I did discover your 'Wheel Freedom' file and a very nice man came and took the wheelchair away.

At least Ian and Jayne look set to remain in London for a while. The situation has delayed their plan to sell their house and move to the country. Jayne has unloaded the contents of her warehouse into their house. Our next-door neighbours are still around, to my surprise, but the others have all fled London for the duration.

In your end of life notes, you asked that your remaining paintings be sold for whatever people could pay rather than market prices. I had arranged with the local pub to hold an exhibition of them in May. You sold so many in that space before, when in 2015 you gave up your studio in Tottenham and moved into the studio you had lovingly built to your specification in the back garden. The May date has had to be cancelled but will take place as soon as coronavirus restrictions are lifted. Proceeds will go to the charity set up by our neighbour to help young boys and men in the East End. There are a great many paintings left, so I do hope I can manage this before damp and mould get to them where they are stored in the garage.

It is weird, but writing this letter to you has brought me profound con-solation. You were such a special person and although you are no longer here, writing makes me feel connected. On the famous day we met in the Manchester wine bar – Cellar Vie! – you appeared to be a typical middle-aged, middle-class, slightly provincial businessman in your smart suit, with glass and cigarette in hand. How wrong I was. As we peeled away your onion layers, the real John slowly came into view, a man who was artistic, clever, passionate, caring as well as well versed in the manly arts of gardening, DIY, shoe- and silver-polishing. You loved me as I had never been loved. And I returned that love for more than forty years. You are missed by many but most sorely by me. I talk to you every day. I am doing my best, my darling.

Love,
Anne

Chapter 4: Aftermath

Grief not only takes many forms. It also attaches to many things: to pets and possessions, to strangers as well as the people closest to us. To opportunities lost and those that never came or never will come again. To break-ups, breakdowns, breakages. To miscarriages of justice and miscarriages. To innocence lost and the beings we once were, whole and unscarred and carefree. To finality.

We sometimes feel ashamed of lesser griefs, as if sadness for a loved animal or a broken dream lacks legitimacy. People have apologised to me, too, for weeping over Andy, fearful that only partners and family members are fully entitled to grieve. Grief can neither be policed, nor should be. I may not have appreciated the call from Andy's fan the day after he died, but I would never question the authenticity of the emotions that prompted him to dial my number. Grief for someone you don't know often incorporates a sense memory of deeper losses. The lives of public figures provide milestones for others. Perhaps a Gang of Four song sound-tracked a significant event for this man, love or death. Maybe he wanted to relive a vibrant instant, flinging himself into the memory of a mosh pit. Above him, Andy, eyes narrowed, swings his guitar like a scythe.

I remember Andy's own grief for the people closest to him:

for his mother, for Auntie June, for his father, for Yannis and Michael and Paula and Peaches and Sarah and Sara B and Maurice. I remember his grief, so recent and raw, for John. I think, too, of other losses. There's a framed photograph on the wall outside our bedroom of Jimmy Hendrix, whose playing inspired Andy and whose death, at 27, shocked him. The picture was a birthday present from Andy's former manager, Jazz Summers. They enjoyed each other's company, those two, Jazz dropping anecdotes like beats, about his times in the army or tours with Wham!, Andy, doing something that for all his wit and exuberance he did better than most: listening. During his final illness, Jazz asked Andy to visit. Andy, to his eternal regret, was slow off the mark. When he called to make arrangements, someone else answered the phone. Jazz had died that morning.

I think, too, of the car Andy lovingly tended for years, a gold-coloured Mercedes SL, the early Seventies model with a metal roof that could be winched off the chassis to reveal a retractable canvas top. One day, I found Andy in the studio and sensed, from his posture, that he was upset. 'What's wrong?', I asked. He looked up from the mixing desk with a miserable expression. He'd sold the car – so much effort it took to maintain it and the metal roof needed replacing. He'd been trying, without success, to source spare parts. Already he regretted the sale. Call the buyer, I urged. Tell him you've changed your mind. He considered this advice, talked himself in circles, eventually decided he should honour the agreement and, hunched with sadness, drove the car away to meet its new owner. Right up to his death, Andy mourned that car as if it had been a member of our household.

I think of the crowds that line the streets for state funerals, of the unseen woman whose cries pierced the unnatural silence of Princess Diana's cortege. 'My Diana,' she wailed. 'Oh, my Diana.' I think of the gatherings and processions for George Floyd, whose killing by police as the US succumbed to the pandemic spoke to a different contagion, baked into systems and structures, enabled by vested interests to persist and flourish. Thousands travelled to Houston from across America to pay tribute to Floyd, enduring temperatures of over forty degrees to salute his coffin on its journey from the Fountain of Praise church to the cemetery. Thousands more made pilgrimage to the intersection of the Minneapolis thoroughfares 38th and Chicago, where policeman Derek Chauvin had knelt, for eight minutes and forty-six seconds, on Floyd's neck, Chauvin's three colleagues looking on, unmoved and unmoving.

'I can't breathe,' Floyd protested. 'I can't breathe.' So many resonances there are in that phrase that it's easy to lose sight of the man who shaped it with his dying breath. It's easy to lose sight, too, of those who mourn him, not as a symbol of injustice, but a person they knew and loved and relied on and teased and maybe, on occasion, spoke to or about with a flippancy they now regret.

'I can't breathe.' The phrase reverberates through communities stifled by prejudice and discrimination going back generations. It summons the ghosts of the millions of victims of slavery, historical and modern, some named, many more unrecorded, and of the millions more killed by poverty, racism and the complicity of good men who do nothing. It rolls across Beirut, a second shockwave after a huge explosion, preventable and foreseeable, slaughters hundreds and leaves hundreds of thousands homeless. It sounds again and again in the emerging statistics showing higher mortality rates for Covid-19 among Black and Asian populations more likely to work in frontline and ill-protected jobs, and live and commute in crowded spaces. This is a powerful grief, the sorrow and rage of the disempowered, the overpowered. This is a grief both intensely personal and collective.

Mandu Reid, who in becoming leader of the Women's Equality Party chalked up a belated first as the first woman of colour to lead a UK political party, feels she must give public articulation to this grief. When she tries to do so, she understands that Chauvin has stolen her breath too. 'I realised over the weekend that since childhood one of the ways I've learned to cope with the inevitability and ubiquity of racism is by not allowing myself to *really feel* much at all when I'm confronted by it,' she emails me. 'More often than not my default has been to engage with it on a purely intellectual level, or sometimes by trying to minimise my experience of it.' Swiftly she recovers her voice, uses it to make extraordinary speeches and write searing letters, but the process deepens her discomfort. It is part of the grim history of equality movements that the victims of inequality, rather than its generals, are sent again and again into battle, cannon fodder, their pain split open and anatomised and even then dismissed.

'I can't breathe.' It is Andy's complaint in those last days. It is the whispered entreaty of the Covid-19 patients condemned to inferior treatment or none because their lives are deemed of little value. A friend writes to me from the care home where she works without PPE or the reassurance of any kind of testing regime for staff or residents. Hospitals have been told to clear beds to make space for the anticipated influx of coronavirus sufferers; many elderly patients are being bundled off, untested, to care homes. The disease will kill thousands in these institutions and is already taking hold at this one, but my friend has a wider point to make about the ways in which cultural attitudes to the old and disabled play out.

'Care homes,' she muses. 'The name says it all. A place where people are cared for and their needs fulfilled, or even surpassed? Well, that would be a grand reality. The reality is that people in care homes are ticked off the list if their basic needs are being cared for. It is only in this sudden grip of isolation for us all that we may be able to truly understand what it is to be in a care home. Then imagine that, as well as not being able to venture outside, you have your smart phone erased. Your dinners are served lukewarm on a wonky wooden-veneered table while a whipper-snapper strips you naked only to wake you up – uninvited – with a wipe, again lukewarm, which (fingers crossed) has a soapsuds adornment. You hate the mornings, mainly because they are undignified and cold. Very cold. Occasionally the odd goodie comes in beaming and tells you that their warm flannel will be rubbed all over your face in approximately three seconds. Oh, those are the good days.'

At the start of lockdown, the National Institute for Health and Care Excellence – the acronym spells the word 'nice' – issued guidance ahead of an anticipated shortage of critical care beds. All adult patients should be scored for 'frailty'. That score would potentially funnel any Covid-19 patients dependent on others for help towards end-of-life care instead of life-saving critical care. Emergency legislation, passed at the same time, liberated councils from most of their obligations to assess and meet the needs of adults with disabilities. Families of the Covid dead complain that Do Not Resuscitate notices have been imposed on their loved ones, without consultation.

Disdain for the old and disabled is illuminated by Covid, not created by it. Years earlier, my friend Richard falls and breaks his hip. By then in his early forties, his degenerative condition, ataxia, is sufficiently advanced that he can no longer walk. He slips as he manoeuvres between bed and wheelchair. He has been living independently and is fiercely engaged with the world, campaigning on disability rights as well as the iniquity that has been the focus of his working life, flag-of-convenience shipping, a literal vessel for slavery and exploitation.

When I visit Richard in hospital – St Thomas's, the same institution that will give Andy such excellent care – I find him helpless and in pain. It has taken two days for news of his plight to reach me. Since his admission, he has lain ignored in a general ward, no update on the surgery he needs, and little done to alleviate the torment of his shattered pelvis. His meals are deposited on his bedside table; nobody gives him assistance to eat. He is starving and soiled and very frightened.

I intervene, making noise until someone with authority to improve Richard's treatment puts in an appearance. The nurse in charge doesn't deny my allegations. She attempts, instead, to frame this wilful neglect as a form of humanity. She tries to persuade me that Richard no longer has anything to live for.

A few years later, the nurse appears to me in a dream that adds a name badge to her starched chest: Gloria Monday. In real life, Richard is once more in hospital and hoping to be released, but an outbreak of norovirus has delayed his discharge. In my dream, Nurse Monday blocks his departure until an ambulance can be summoned to carry him home. I wheel him to the entrance to wait. Eventually a van draws up. The logo on its side: *Sick Transit Gloria Monday*.

The nurse and her false assumptions about what constitutes a life worth living still haunt my waking hours, whenever the question arises of assisted dying. Richard campaigned for the right to die. I continue to do so. Yet its implementation is complicated in any country that fails to value all of its citizens equally – and that, of course, is every country.

In a column written eight days before the World Health Organization declared the Covid outbreak to be a pandemic, the *Telegraph*'s assistant editor, Jeremy Warner, provided a glimpse of the cultural attitudes that inevitably, and with tragic consequences, informed the UK's response to the virus. 'From an entirely disinterested economic perspective, the Covid-19 might even prove mildly beneficial in the long term by disproportionately culling elderly dependents,' he wrote.

The Office for National Statistics would later calculate that the disabled made up almost two-thirds of UK Covid deaths in a ten-week period at the start of the pandemic. At least twenty-thousand deaths from the virus are confirmed to have taken place in care homes, with the actual totals thought to be significantly higher. The government overruled a plan, early in the pandemic, to restrict movements of staff between care homes and also failed to ensure adequate PPE and other resources for a sector starved long term of investment. These victims weren't simply more vulnerable to Covid. They were made more vulnerable to it.

How should we grieve for those victims deemed less worthy of life, less entitled to our sorrow? Sometimes grief is not a passive state but a call to action. You can keep your tears, your flowers, your Thoughts and Prayers. It is not enough to feel, if feeling fails to translate into movement towards change, however small.

Here's another thing about grief. Its greatest gift is clarity. Of course, it scrambles some circuitry, turns days into one long night. I cannot tell you exactly what I did in the immediate aftermath of Andy's death, yet I had a strong sense of what really mattered – and what really didn't. Grief crowded out petty concerns and set priorities. I couldn't imagine life without Andy, but understood the imperative to create fresh meaning, to use my time well. That clarity endures. Like my unvarnished memories of Andy, I intend to hang on to it for as long as possible.

The effect was enhanced by the behaviours of people around me. During Andy's final illness and in the weeks and months that followed, I saw the absolute best of people and the rancid, near-comically villainous worst. The latter category, thankfully, encompassed a far narrower range, mostly strangers. By proxy, I now worked in the music business, sorting through Andy's complex legacy of compositions and co-writes, recorded performances and production work, mixes, film and TV scores, and tracks yet to be released. The photographer and film maker Anton Corbijn, who met Andy in 1980, on assignment to New York to shoot Gang of Four for the cover of the *NME*, called me with a timely warning. Anton's Dutch accent adds an umlaut to his Us. 'You may be a widow,' he told me, 'but the music industry will fück you over.'

It was useful advice, though most people in the business have defied the stereotype, showing me nothing but courtesy and integrity. Nor was the risk confined to the world of music. Within five days of Andy's death, I dealt with the first of several attempts to open a credit card account in his name. A week later, scammers impersonated him to order items for delivery. After an attempt to break into our flat via the garage, possibly to retrieve these parcels, I fetched from the studio the metal baseball bat the band had used during performances to beat a microwave, creating both a percussive noise and a metaphor.

The bat still lies by Andy's empty side of the bed, ready for non-tropological use against any intruder.

I was also tempted to wield it against my own laptop when Andy's former manager Aaron alerted me to advertisements for commemorative shirts featuring a stylised image of Andy, his torso forming the I of the phrase R.I.P. In other circumstances, I might have dismissed this as merely the latest example of a perennial problem: unauthorised merchandise. At time of writing, one R.I.P.-off merchant is selling a range of items emblazoned with Gang of Four's logo, including, with all the taste associated with such enterprises, face masks.

What distinguished this attempt to monetise Andy's death, apart from its speed – the t-shirt went on sale days after he died – was its marketing. Those advertisements, splattered across social media, hooked potential customers with a picture digitally altered to appear as if Gang of Four's bass player, Thomas, wore, and endorsed, the shirt. 'See You Again My Friend,' read the legend. Facebook algorithms, with the remorseless logic of machine intelligence, targeted the people most likely to be interested – Gang of Four fans, our friends, families, me and, inevitably, Thomas himself: Thomas, who so recently balanced on the window sill overnight in the ICU, rather than leave Andy's side; Thomas, who loved Andy, watched out for Andy, who had just lost, at a stroke, his dear friend and a big part of his future. 'That's a fuckin' low move,' he WhatsApped me, with touching restraint. We tried and failed to get the adverts taken down.

The publicity around Andy's death, combined with the potential market for souvenirs, made us a particularly attractive prospect for creeps and fraudsters, but the bereaved are always at heightened risk. Common scams directed at the newly grief-stricken include posing as a debt collector and threatening to seize assets to settle the deceased's mythical unpaid bill. Fake brokers dangle fictitious life insurance policies that will supposedly pay out on receipt of a final missing premium. A variant of that trick promises, in return for an administrative fee, documents essential to completing probate. Anyone who has scrambled to assemble the paperwork of sadmin will understand the temptation to take up any offers of help going.

I avoided these traps. My mother did not. One day, worried because I couldn't get through on her landline, I reached her on her mobile instead. She dislikes and rarely answers it, so I knew something must be wrong. She told me she'd been speaking all morning to an 'anti-fraud organisation' that had rung to warn her of the theft of six hundred pounds from her bank account; she had to keep the landline free for their return call. They are not helping you with fraud, they are the fraudsters, I told her. By then she had provided details of accounts at two separate banks, her telecoms package and mobile number and email address. Lise and I headed over, ringing the banks and internet service provider on the way. I also alerted the police. This would be Lise's first time inside our mother's house since lockdown. We had been hypervigilant in protecting our mother against Covid, but neglected to shield her from this older disease. How should she, fresh as she was to the world of remote transactions, recognise the danger signals? Before Covid, she did her banking and shopping in person.

The fraudsters won her trust because they already had some of her personal details. As the call dragged on, she became restive, challenging them to prove who they were. They told her 'If you don't believe us, just hang up'. In the following days, upset and off balance, much of her new-won confidence destroyed, she would wonder how they had come to target her. We can't know, but this much is certain: obituaries and death notices provide rich sources of data to identity fraudsters and burglars. Despite this, newspapers insist on carrying unnecessary details, such as exact dates and locations of birth and death. *The Gazette*, the official journal of record in the UK, goes a step further, printing the full street address of the dead in statutory notices intended to give creditors a chance to submit bills to estates before any disbursements to beneficiaries. My solicitor, aware that Andy's estate had already been targeted by criminals, asked the editors of *The Gazette* to consider publishing such a notice complete but for our flat number. They refused.

As Lise and I waited for the police, our mother told us, almost casually, that someone had tried to break in the previous night, while she slept. I went outside and saw that her garage door, just like mine, had been crowbarred partially open.

My mother seemed less distressed by the old-style crime, and I could understand why. For someone as emotionally self-sufficient as she had been, reliant on my stepfather but otherwise contained, a big part of her adjustment to widowhood involves learning to rely on other people, to trust them. The fraudsters persuaded her they were helping her. All fraud is cruel, but the weaponising of bereavement deserves a special place in hell.

People, like grief, can be awful. Happily, they seem more often inclined to demonstrate another of grief's facets: love. The kindness of friends, family and total strangers sustained me through the days and nights at St Thomas's and continues to do so.

Some of that sustenance came in a direct and essential form. All of us tried to coax Andy to eat, but he struggled to swallow the meals and protein drinks provided by hospital catering.

Nothing tastes of anything, he complained. One friend exulted after the manchego cheese and membrillo he brought briefly revived Andy's appetite. Noting this small victory, the nursing staff asked me, in contravention of usual guidelines, to cook for Andy. Better that he should risk meals prepared in a private kitchen than fade away. I ran straight home to make almond soup with grapes marinated in sherry vinegar. The previous summer, after our stay in Spain, we'd gone on a cold-soup kick, addicted to this dish, *ajo blanco*, and to red gazpacho and *salmorejo*. He managed only a single spoonful.

After they put him under, I pretty much stopped eating too. Grief dulls every form of hunger but the one it represents. At the hospital, my dining choices were limited to sandwiches and salads too refrigerated to taste; once home, the idea of baring a tear-swollen face at the shops felt daunting. Cooking, for a while, was anyway off limits. It made no sense without Andy. Food had been central to our relationship, our passion and pursuit. Every oblong of stock in our freezer either carried a label designed by him to denote fish or meat – a blue fish, a brown cow – or if lacking a label recalled frequent, laughing skirmishes over whose responsibility the labelling should have been. Every oblong preserved the molecules of meals we had made and eaten together. We always froze leftovers until we had enough for the alchemy of stock-making. I had simmered up two particularly rich stocks one sleepless night as Andy lay dying, one from the remnants of the Christmas dinner we hosted after John's death, the other with fish bought just before Andy's admission to hospital in mid-January, when I hoped to tempt him into eating by preparing some of his favourite dishes. I labelled the stocks as soon as they iced over.

Perceptive friends didn't bother to ask if there was anything

I needed. Instead they brought what I didn't know I needed, containers of soup and home-cooked dinners, delicious breads and snacks. Jo stocked my larder and fridge for weeks and still sends me care packages, three perfect artichokes and a steady supply of the granola she bakes, christened 'crackola' for its addictive qualities. One of her best gifts was a map of London's historic trees. My lonely lockdown walks became quests, each day a new destination, an old tree.

Memories of generosity stand out, diamond-like on the velvet blur of passing days. The people who kept vigil for Andy on the rare occasions I couldn't be at his bedside, the friends who volunteered to drive me across London on the saddest of errands. The rebel forces who smuggled contraband into the hospital.

The smuggling operation started after a nurse summoned me to the family room. I could guess what the summons must mean. Medical staff with serious faces lay out poor prognoses for assembled families on these leatherette benches. At this stage, Andy was still expected to recover. I steeled myself against unconscionable news.

The nurse's stern expression reinforced my fears but when she spoke it was not about Andy. Someone had seen me in this very room *with a can of beer*. Yes, I agreed. I like to have a beer with my evening meal. It occurred to me, as I spoke, that the brand, Dead Pony, may have offended. The infringement turned out to be more egregious: alcohol was not allowed on the premises.

I agreed to mend my ways, but friends had other ideas. Suddenly I developed what looked like a late-night coffee habit, actually a steady supply of pale ale decanted into Costa Coffee cups.

The nurse had done her job, my friends were doing theirs. And the hospital staff not only performed the roles for which they were contracted but far exceeded them in offering support too. How much grief must cloud their working lives, these brilliant ICU staff whose patients would not be under their care if death were not an urgent possibility and frequent outcome? Even so, they dig deep. So many small things they do to try to alleviate fear and pain. There is a nurse watching over Andy at all times, a one-to-one ratio. They are highly trained and informed by experience, picking up on the smallest signs, making the most delicate of adjustments, to the instruments or the angle of his body.

We get to know all of them and the catering staff. Every day a man brings a menu round, reads it out though it never changes, and talks to Andy about his homeland, Brazil. He is entranced to discover that Andy has played in parts of the country rarely visited by tourists. Inevitably they discuss Brazilian cooking too. He tries so hard, this man, to find something that Andy will eat, looks crestfallen when he comes to clear the dishes and finds them as he left them.

At the far end of the ICU, a woman lies in a section screened off from the rest of the ward by glass. She is dying in her own sweet time, attended by four generations of her large family, who congregate every day, in different constellations, in the family room. One morning her granddaughter seeks me out. She carries her baby in the crook of one arm and in her opposite hand a paper bag containing a coffee and a pastry. 'I thought you needed something to eat,' she says.

An hour after Andy dies, she stops me in the corridor to give me a sympathy card. We have stayed in touch and would have attended the ceremonies for each other's loved one but for the coincidence of dates. Just one day separates the funeral for her grandmother and Andy's memorial.

More recently she texts to suggest meeting up. 'You've been on my mind lately,' she writes. 'I know it's been a rubbish year, but I hope you're managing to keep somewhat of a happy outlook on life at this moment. In these uncertain times I take comfort from happy memories of past smiles and sunny days, I hope you can too.'

The second letter to John

20 April 2020

Dear John,

You would have been 84 today and I wanted to write to you again. You loved birthdays and we always celebrated. I finally came out about my real age when I held my huge seventieth at the Foreign Press Association. Your eightieth at the Athenaeum Club was a memorable night for many reasons. You were so robust and glowing that it is difficult to believe that was only four years ago. Your daughter Sarah, in remission from ovarian cancer, gave the speech of her lifetime. The next morning she married her second husband and not six months later she died.

It's not even a month since my last letter, so this one will probably be considerably shorter. There is not much to report when one is under house arrest and one day much like another. However, in a very pleasant surprise, my routine this afternoon was interrupted by Cheryl and Alistair, who cycled over with a bottle of fizz to celebrate your birthday. The day was gorgeous, and we were soon joined by Ian and Jayne. As strict quarantine is still in place, we stood at the corners of the front garden and outside the gate, toasting you with fizz in tea mugs and paper cups with me beneath the giant echium. You would have loved it and were entirely there in spirit.

Today is also Florence's birthday and she is 20. It seems only days ago when we received that telephone call from Catherine A and Keith in Marrakesh to say your granddaughter had been born on your birthday. The four Andersons are observing lockdown strictly and not going outside their front door, so it may be months before I see them again. That is the very worst thing about the pandemic; being cut off from people and there seems no end in sight. We are in the fifth week of lockdown already. Life is not impossible, but it is very hard.

Back to the Andersons for a moment. I told you in my last letter that Keith's father George, whose dementia has become very serious, fell and broke his hip. Poor George woke up in hospital with no understanding of where he was or what had happened. After three weeks on a ward, he was suddenly moved without consent or warning to a care home. Sadly, care homes are now nests of infection; over three quarters of all the care homes in the UK are losing serious numbers of their patients to the virus. So, who knows what George's chances are. His wife Lita is locked down alone and not allowed to see him; Keith is not permitted to visit either of his parents.

It must be very tough for all of them. At least the rest of the family have kept well so far. In a pandemic which is ravaging the whole world, the UK, which was very late off the starting blocks in preparation, planning and warning the population, stands to have the most deaths from coronavirus of any country in Europe. This is astonishing, as both Italy and Spain seemed in the bidding for that honour. The disease first took European root in northern Italy and claimed thousands of lives there. Spain has suffered a similar catastrophe but in the UK, we are catching them up fast.

As you were a dedicated hospital governor, you will be able to imagine the chaos in hospitals. Coronavirus, now known by the specific strain, Covid-19, is a disease which you can have so lightly that you hardly know you are ill, or so seriously that you cannot survive, but its main effect is very similar to the symptoms you and Andy lived and died with, extreme difficulty in breathing. The virus damages the lungs in a terrible way and there are not enough beds, ventilators, personnel or protective clothing and masks. Woe betide anybody who has anything else wrong and needs medical help.

As with any pandemic, the famous and prominent do not escape. I mentioned in my last letter that Prince Charles and Boris Johnson had caught it. Charles had Covid-19 lightly. Johnson, on the other hand, nearly died and spent a week in ICU at St. Thomas's, where we said goodbye to Andy. The elderly are being treated as its natural victims but in reality survivors include a woman of 103 and our friend Blanche, approaching 96, while a 13-year-old boy died the other day and many in their twenties and thirties. The race is on for a vaccine, and rumour has it that anyone over 75 will not be let out of lockdown until they find one – in eighteen months or two years.

I cannot let myself dwell on that prospect. It is bad enough that I have just finished four weeks of lockdown and have been told that we will continue for another three weeks at least. Facing this on my own is not proving easy. As you well remember, I am an anxious person who wants to know what is round the corner, and a controlling one, who wants to be in charge. You were always so adept in calming me down and making me see things in some sort of proportion, which would have been so amazingly helpful in this situation. We all just have to take each day as it comes, and when you are locked up, one day is very much like another.

If I have a saving grace, it is my love for routine. I do my housework as always (certain rooms on certain days). I collect Elizabeth's and my newspapers at 10 (our normal newsagent shut down), take a one-hour walk at lunchtime, and go for the *Evening Standard* about 4 p.m. It is so slim now, with no sports or arts news, that our journalist friend Matt calls it *The Evening Pamphlet,* but it still has good crossword puzzles. I can only do the Quick Crosswords; if you were here we would be working together on the Cryptics and mastering them. We would be doing all sorts of things together, as we always did, and I particularly miss Scrabble, which whiled away many an hour after your illness set in. More than that, I miss conversation; your thoughts and ideas were always interesting and, like everything else in your life, you never shied away from forceful opinions.

Having seen you, in your illness, drift into TV from lunchtime onwards, I made a strict rule after you died not to ever turn the television on before 8 p.m. And I have stuck to it, although I do admit to watching every evening as it is one of the only things which really takes me out of myself. And I still listen faithfully to *The Archers*, although coronavirus has not yet reached Ambridge! I am writing too – not only these letters to you but a weekly blog for a new website set up by Carole and her friend Lucia and aimed at women over 50. I am representing the older end of that age group and have delivered three blogs and am writing the fourth now. This is a really good project for me as it has got me writing and thinking outside the box and they seem pleased with my efforts so far.

It is painful not to be able to see the family in person but the Mayer end of it has a weekly dinner on Zoom on Friday evenings. Catherine A and Keith have been invited to join us but haven't yet been free to do so. But Catherine, Cassie, Lise, Isaac and his now live-in girlfriend, David and Helen all join in. It is a good way to connect. Lise gave me an iPad and she and Catherine are both encouraging my progress into the world of technology. I am now on Facebook, although never have time to play with it, and am slowly coming to terms with my smartphone.

Catherine, who is struggling as I am with widowhood, cooks delicious meals for me and walks over to deliver them. All the girls are concerned that I pay too little attention to my health and am too liberal about going outside; I insist, for instance, on doing my own shopping although not at Sainsbury but at the new M&S, which is better organised. We usually have to queue for quite some time as they only let a limited number into the store, but the shelves are well stocked, whereas many supermarkets have been stripped bare by panic buying. And I must tack on here a small tribute to Jane, who turned up this morning with a fish pie to brighten my limited menu; she and

David, good friends that they are, invited me to dinner before lockdown and I extravagantly admired her fish pie, a dish I really love.

Friends have been more than kind, those who are still around and did not flee to the country for the duration. Ian and Jayne watch out for me and do all they can. Next door have been very caring and I love watching the boys playing in the garden from our bedroom window. Elizabeth has been magnificent, but I have had to restrain her from insisting on doing our gardening. Pasquale, who wept at the news of your death, is again caring for the front garden as he does not have to come into the house to do it, but the back garden is a bit of a mess. Over the Easter weekend, when next door knew I was out for my daily walk, they lowered their 9-year-old and the power mower over the fence and instructed him from a distance in how to mow the lawn. It was not exactly perfect, but a wonderful achievement for such a young boy. The echium which Pasquale planted outside our front door, now reaches almost to the upstairs windows and is covered with beautiful tiny purple flowers and buzzing with bees.

In fact, one of the good and unexpected effects of lockdown is nature itself, flourishing as never before. The blossoms on fruit trees and flowers are exceptional and birdsong is loud and clear without traffic noise. You will be delighted that pollution has gone down by more than half. You wanted to save the environment for all of us but you also realised that with your severe lung problems, living in London was literally killing you. What isn't so good is the number of people riding bikes where they shouldn't or breaking all the rules about social interaction that tell us to stay two metres apart and refrain from lingering in parks and on benches. And for everybody who is inspired to be kind and generous, there are those filled with anger and aggression. I can say that from my own experience of being called ugly names, but at least I have the luxury of space. There are many locked down together in small flats with nowhere to retreat.

Probate continues – and continues to be difficult. Most bank branches are closed and telephone-answering staff have been pared to a minimum. It is as if the whole nation is holding its breath and the inevitable consequence of weeks without shops and shopping, travel or commerce of any kind will be a whopping recession, perhaps a depression. And this is even more true of the USA, which has been very badly hit. So I am in almost daily touch with the bank and the solicitor about how to structure my future. A learning curve to be sure. Your car still sits in the garage and your scooter in the big room. No one is buying anything and even if they wanted to, could not come to see or test it. You don't realise how problematic it is not to be able to avail yourself of services until you cannot; one of my teeth is falling out and semi-infected and there is no way I can see a dentist for weeks and weeks. Just to give you an example.

This supposedly short letter is getting longer and longer as there are so many things I realise that I want you to know. I have just endured Easter weekend. It brought back painful but treasured memories of our last Easter together. If you remember, the weather was gorgeous and on Friday we went to the Academy of Ancient Music concert at the Barbican. You had recently become a patron of the Academy and they were reviving Handel's *Brockes-Passion* for the first time in about three hundred years. The four-hour concert did me in, but you were rapt and attentive for every moment of it. On Saturday, your birthday, we had a dinner party; on Sunday we had lunch with Jayne and Ian and on Easter Monday we had that amazing family party in the back garden with all the children and grandchildren and our Danish friend Birthe. This year the weather was fine on Friday and Saturday but turned cold and ugly on Sunday and Monday and I had to fight off despair at what I had lost and the thought of living a life of memories instead of present joy and delight. What I did do on Easter Monday was clear out your desk drawers; a living museum of such variety and now the contents of two large green rubbish bags. Ian is going through various watches, compasses, cameras and oddities for me and eventually I will let your daughter be the arbiter of what remains. Were you to magically return, I would teach you to distinguish a drawer from a waste bin! But it was a strangely cathartic thing to do on a desperate day.

And finally, a shared thought about what will happen if and when the virus finally goes. We will have lived through an experience which hasn't happened since the plague in the Middle Ages, despite all the advances of modern science and medicine. The shops may reopen but life will not return to normal, assuming we can even decide what normal is. They are already talking about blocking off seats on planes and trains and buses and tubes so no one can ever sit next to each other, and that is if a global financial depression doesn't kill off some of those industries anyway. Budget flights and holidays seem a thing of the past and travel in general will take a long time to resume and recover. How long will it be before we cheerfully pack into a pub to watch football or don't mind our table at a crowded restaurant being less than two metres from the next? Will we have to wear face masks in public? A debate rages even as I write.

We won't be the same people and that is for sure. But I am trying very hard to be strong for you, my darling. Not to panic or try to look around too many corners. To remember to be kind and generous even when the floor seems to have given way. And to remember how fortunate I am to have spent more than forty years with you. If, as we once thought when I had cancer, I was the one who was gone and you the one remembering, I am sure you would equally be celebrating our life together and missing me as much as I do you.

Happy birthday!
Love,
Anne

Chapter 5: Three funerals and a memorial

Stop the seconds' flow
Oh, I'm too late
I'm back where I began at the start
I'm caught in the wake
I'll have my due and drag the rock up the hill
Nothing to lose that's not been lost
I wish the sun anchored still
What I wanted disappears in the haze
A speck of dust held forever in the dying rays
Breath on the mirror; nothing inside
The horizon's bare, but in the night, I miss the pilot's light
Control and power, empires were built in our minds
But it will all go up in a blaze; only dust in the dying rays

'The Dying Rays' by Andy Gill

How you remember the lovely dead is not the same as how you memorialise them. Memories are always with us, tendrils that curl into the living moment. Andy has never left and will never leave. Just as in a good marriage, he sometimes fills my vision, at other times stands to one side. We talk, often, and if the conversations are a little one-sided, that's also nothing new. I come from a big, noisy, verbal family. Visits to his mother Sylvia illuminated how different was his background. A couple of hours it took to drive to her house and once there, Andy would sit with her in the front room, often in a silence that I felt compelled to puncture. Yet there was nothing awkward about it, no hostility. On the contrary, mother and son were perfectly at ease, speaking only if moved to do so.

Memorialising, like their way of communicating, is a process of choice, quite distinct from the unregulated splurge of memory. In planning a memorial, we take decisions about how our loved ones should be remembered, though our control over that remembrance will inevitably be limited. Philip Larkin's poem, 'An Arundel Tomb', tells the story of changing percep-tions of a memorial to a long-dead couple. The elements and composition of the tomb assert the aristocratic status of the pair interred within, but the passage of time has stripped the symbols of their intended meaning. Onlookers now see an image of fidelity in death, a man and a woman lying together in effigy and for eternity. 'What will survive of us,' the poem concludes, 'is love.'

Too many funeral services not only end without original meaning; they start that way, all form and formula and few inti-mations of the love at their core. Not that form and formula are without their uses. Religion, as discussed later in this book, provides frameworks and systems for thinking about death and off-the-shelf ways to mark it. I first realised how useful these might be when I found myself, in the middle of a Chicago cemetery, staring from a ceramic pot containing the ashes of my maternal grandmother to the blank faces of my mother, John and other mourners. They had failed to decide in advance what to do at the graveside. Grandma Ruth disapproved of organised religion; its absence led to funereal disorganisation and this wasn't the only moment of comedy. One of Ruth's contemporaries, too ill and demented to join us at the grave, stayed in the car and watched from a distance. Later, at the funeral lunch, he piped up: 'Did anyone get any good photos of the wedding?'

Yet organised religion will often overwrite the dead with its own values and prejudices. I recently stifled an involuntary protest during the funeral of a friend who rose high in the boy's club of journalism to hear her praised not for this or her prodigious heart but in terms set out in Proverbs 31: 10–31 'Who can find a virtuous woman? For her price is far above rubies. The heart of her husband doth safely trust in her, so that he shall have no need of spoil.'

Mismatches between the deceased and the sermon are commonplace; so too is a vacuum where the person should be. 'We are gathered here today to remember so-and-so,' intone priests and vicars and rabbis and imams and celebrants from other faiths and none. Often the speaker possesses not a single direct memory of so-and-so, relying instead on second-hand anecdotage and reciting the deceased's achievements with all the conviction of a recruitment consultant reading through a CV. Then, if a cremation – the final disposition for 75 per cent of Britons, though forbidden under some religions – comes the banality of the rattling fairground ride of coffin on conveyor belt to a backstage area where it will be held for later incineration. It takes up to three hours for the coffin and its cargo to burn. 'They don't mix the ashes from different cremations,' the funeral director volunteers, as we stand outside the East Chapel at Golders Green Crematorium. 'In case you're wondering. The ashes you get will all come from Andrew.'

'And his coffin,' I reply, ever the pedant. I am pretty sure that I hear Andy groan. I stare at the plate on the door, with a slot for the name. On this Valentine's morning, it reads: *Reserved for Service to the Late ANDREW JAMES DALYRYMPLE GILL.* The late Andrew Gill. Finally it's official. My beloved is famed and feared for his ability to turn up late for planes and trains and occasions big and small. Today he has no option but to be punctual. The funeral director drove him here. I travelled separately, by tube, with one of his best friends, Emma. His brother Martin joins us. We three will be the only mourners – and there won't be a service. Andy and I edited our wedding vows to minimalist perfection – did we take each other, to love and to cherish, in health and in sickness? Yes, we did. In an unconscious echo of that happy day, I have blue-pencilled his funeral. Back then, we reserved our energies for the delicious raucousness of the party that followed our exchange of vows. Now I hold fire for the memorial. Today there will be no empty words. There will be no words at all.

Inside the chapel we wait, one last time, for Andy. Six pall-bearers bring him in. His is the cheapest veneer coffin on the funeral director's list. I would have gone for a greener option, but the cardboard and wicker versions I'm shown are pricey, and I lacked the energy to shop around. The shape and dimensions of the casket are close to Andy's own. Of course. I should have expected this. When I walk to the front and embrace it, I embrace him, live again that last embrace at the hospital, as one-sided as our conversations have become.

I spend a few minutes hugging him, then step aside for Emma and Martin. At some point, we turn tear-streaked faces to each other and know we are ready to leave. I have requested that he remain in place while we do so. No fairground ride for Andy. I thank the funeral director and then walk back down the hill with the others, towards the tube station. One of Andy's songs runs through my head. Called 'The Dying Rays', he originally recorded it for a Gang of Four album five years earlier. After his death, the band created a new version. We have today released it, the first single from a commemorative EP, *This Heaven Gives Me Migraine*. The main image on the EP will be a photograph taken by Anton Corbijn back in the early Eighties, Andy asleep on a bed, spread-eagled, legs dangling, a smile on his face, a beatific Thomas Chatterton.

This is my Valentine to Andy and the beginning of a process of memorialising that will consist of many elements and may last for years. In private, I hold tight to the Andy I know. Out in the world, I choose which aspects to share. He may be dead, but he shall not fade. I come to précis Andy, not to bury him. (Yes, my darling, I heard you groan at that too.) None of this offers much comfort, but it is the only thing I can still do for him.

The best ceremonies flow from a close and affectionate knowledge of the loved one they are designed to celebrate. No amount of money can buy you a good funeral if the personal element is missing. Horse-drawn carriages will as likely distract from the deceased as reflect a life lived, unless he or she was an equestrian – or a gangster. A Promethean casket – gold-plated, with fully adjustable bed and blue velvet interior – will certainly speak to the wealth of its inhabitant, retailing, as it does, for $24,000. The coffin of choice for James Brown and Michael Jackson, it is also proof that no amount of burnished metal can burnish a reputation.

The funeral director who handled Andy's 'simple cremation' worried when first I informed him of my no-frills choice. It was fine to transport Andy to Golders Green in a van rather than a hearse, I said. He had, after all, spent much of his life in splitter vans and cronky tour buses. The funeral director explained he was trying to protect me against negative press. He'd seen the obituaries for Andy, knew that newspapers trawled crematoria for details of forthcoming funerals and feared paparazzi at the gates, snapping Andy being offloaded with all the dignity of a metal flight case from one of those tour buses. I knew the advice came from a good place, but I didn't take it. While some undertakers push customers towards expensive flourishes to swell their margins, I trusted this one. Three years earlier, he'd helped stage Sara B's funeral. Just eleven days ago, he and his colleagues had done my stepfather proud. I just figured Andy wouldn't – and couldn't – care.

No such guesswork was necessary with Sara B. She and I discussed her funeral often and in detail during her final lingering. In pain and depleted, this was the difficult death she had feared, but her children, Lili and Reuben, enabled a little quality of life almost to the end by tending to her at home. They created a daytime perch for her, a hospital bed, disguised with colourful throws and cushions. There she would sit or lie, her mini-Schnauzer Smudge at her feet. Lise organised a dog-walking rota. One distracted day during my turn, I failed to notice Smudge lift a leg on railings until I heard outraged cries from below. Canine urine, with great precision, arced onto the helmet of a contractor working in the lightwell of the property.

I performed better at the other functions Sara B entrusted to me. She drew up a Lasting Power of Attorney for Health and Welfare in case she became too incapacitated to take decisions, potentially forcing her son and daughter, both in their twenties, to wrestle unaided with the question of removing life support. I was her third 'attorney' and arbiter in case of any split decisions. She also appointed me her gatekeeper. Well-meaning friends flocked to her bedside and, finding her mute with exhaustion, nevertheless stayed for hours. She asked me to allocate slots and insist on prompt departures.

Her third request related to the funeral: I should work with Lili and Reuben to realise her ideas for it. She was an artist and designer. Her visual sense was highly developed, both a superpower and a liability that left her flinching at tiny infelicities others couldn't even see. Her aesthetic – bold and vivid – reflected her personality. Her funeral shouldn't merely give testimony to those characteristics; it had to embody them.

Such details really mattered to her, but our conversations also gave us an easy way to talk about the reality of her situation. We pored over photographs of 'proverb boxes', Ghanaian coffins sculpted into items of significance for the deceased. She exclaimed over a giant pink grouper, a jet painted in the colours of the national carrier, a Nikon camera. A casket modelled on a box of Marlboro made her laugh. 'I'll bet Philip Morris International aren't too keen on this one.'

She never saw the coffin that, in both senses, fully captured her. Painted by the artist Jenkin van Zyl, a family friend, she appeared on the lid in near full-sized portrait, winged, with a gown of stars, standing on a verdant planet earth, the sun above her head, and emblazoned with a single word, 'Buttzilla', Lili and Reuben's nickname for her. She was present in every other aspect of the ceremony, too. Guests, arriving at St Marylebone Crematorium, the prettiest of London's facilities, collected Mardi Gras beads on the way in; friends and family contributed stories about her; and her sister performed the whooping pig call they had both perfected as the daughters of an Arkansas farmer. It had always delighted us to persuade Sara B to make this call. A woman of almost alienating beauty, she happily played against the grain of expectation this forced on her.

Her children found a humanist celebrant, Nicci Gerrard, who spent a good few hours with us, talking about her and planning the shape of the celebration. The tight timetables of crematoria can lend a municipal impersonality to proceedings, one in, one out, seven-and-a-half minutes to get everyone seated, forty-five for the service, another seven-and-a-half minutes to exit. We booked a double slot and worked with Nicci on a script that gently dissuaded the speakers from derailing the timings. She warned that nerves and emotions might anyway intervene. Not everyone is articulate in the grips of grief, but not to worry, she said. Grief, itself, speaks volumes.

Nicci also presides over John's funeral. It is a chill afternoon, with an edge of rain. I cannot know that I will return to this place for Andy's funeral in less than two weeks, but unease seeps into my bones. Right now my love still speaks, still breathes and I'm missing unmissable time with him, stranded on the wrong side of London with my unspeakable fears. Yet to go to him is not an option. I must support my mother, and, beyond that, I want to be here, for John. Step-parents, like widows, are the go-to villains of popular culture, but mine from the outset defied the stereotypes. I would have embraced John and Helen for making my parents happy, but they came to mean much more. I loved John. I love Helen. I love the way they transformed the dynamics of our family. Families have fixed ideas and reflexes. My stepmother and stepfather opened ours up, showed us different, better ways to be. John also introduced his daughters into our lives. I will always be grateful for that too.

Quickly my stepsisters and I became close. After Sarah moved to London, we became closer still. Her death, at 52, changed John. A bluff, barrel-chested man, brimming with good humour, overnight he curved over and inwards, as if not only the ribs had shrunk but the heart within. It is a very particular grief, he said, to lose a child, against the natural order.

This was the only real conversation we had about Sarah's loss, on the day she died, even though she had been ill for more than a year. My mother remarked recently that John and Andy had more in common than their joy of life; they shared, too, its mirror image, a horror of death. She could never fully break through John's reserve. It was her friend Joanie, a volunteer with an organisation called Gentle Dusk, set up to dismantle taboos and promote better preparedness for death and grief, who persuaded John to complete a detailed end of life plan. By then John was aware that his conditions were incurable.

After his death, my mother found his instructions, in handwriting as cramped as his spirit had been open. It was by then too late to follow them to the letter, but the document still proved useful, helping to set the tone for his funeral and establish which points of his biography John himself considered significant. It included, to our surprise, a proposal that his funeral be held in a local church he had never attended as a congregant. We decided to stick with the arrangement we had already made – the West Chapel at Golders Green accommodates 160 mourners with an overspill area for a further hundred; we correctly predicted a large turnout for John in consonance with the yawning gap he had left in many lives. John would get his religious remembrance at a future date. He had asked that his ashes be taken to Salisbury Cathedral, where as a young boy he had served as a chorister.

So here we are. John's admirers fill every seat and still they file in, crowding by the doorway two and three deep. I watch Catherine A as she gives instructions to the musicians she found for the service, marvelling at her composure. It is only three years since Sarah's funeral and her death came on the heels of losing their mother. If losing parents is the definition and start of true adulthood, as some insist, then give me perpetual adolescence. My parents' great ages are a source of wonderment and terror. If I believed in God, I would pray: no more losses, dear lord. No more.

My father and Helen, down from Manchester for the occasion, take their seats. My mother, outwardly calm, greets guests. Catherine A musters her children and Isaac into a pew near the lectern. They will give readings, as will Sarah's eldest daughter. We have included works by William Golding, John's schoolteacher and lifelong inspiration. I clutch a sheet of paper, my mother's tribute.

I feel reasonably confident of delivering her words dry-eyed, but reckon without the powerful eulogy composed by her friend Ian, who speaks just before me. A self-styled curmudgeon, he lowers our defences by playing up to this image, declaring 'those who know me understand that I loathe 98 per cent of humanity with a vengeance'. We are unguarded when he changes tack to talk, movingly and fluently, of love. 'I always told John that I didn't believe in life after death and God but that I did believe in life before death and I did believe in good,' Ian concludes. 'He exemplified both and was one of the very few people I would say was a hero of mine. It's unlikely, but if I ever get to 80 without being murdered, I want to be like John Bird.'

*

By the time Andy's memorial approaches, politicians are debating tough measures against Covid. Big fixtures and gatherings are cancelled or postponed, though not in the UK. Quarantines and states of emergency are imposed, though not in the UK. The first European country to fully lock down is Italy, on 9 March. I am convinced that governments should and must act swiftly. How can I not be, when so recently I witnessed the impotence of medical interventions in the face of an unyielding virus? Already I beg people to keep their distance. There would anyway be little relief in an embrace that is not the one I crave. I have no fear for my own health but the idea that I might inadvertently carry the sickness to someone else, especially my mother, haunts me.

A related concern troubles my sleep or would if I slept. My body is more insubstantial than ashes, makes no demands of me. Only my thoughts weigh me down. What if we have to cancel? Close to four hundred people are due to attend the memorial event we are organising at London's Conway Hall, friends and family flying in from as far afield as California. This has been my focus and fixation since Andy died. I live for the prospect of a celebration of him, for him, by him. (We plan to bring him to life in films and recordings.) In the end, the memorial goes ahead on 4 March and two nights before that I perform, in the same space, my piece about Paula to an audience of a similar size, as part of a fundraiser for the Primadonna Festival which I co-founded. I recall almost nothing of that evening, except that I didn't get through the piece without crying.

Be careful what you wish for. A scientist who advises the government in the early stages of the crisis later tells a parliamentary committee that a swifter lockdown could have halved the numbers of lives lost. Instead the UK stays open throughout this period and hindsight tells me that the Primadonna fundraiser and Andy's memorial were both probably vectors of infection.

This is the strangest of the strangest times, at the dawn of pandemic and of grief, personal and public. I yearn for touch and shrink from it. I grapple with how best to memorialise my sweetheart while the world grows befuddled with death. How quickly people become statistics, as if the human brain cannot conceive of tragedies at scale. War dead, famine dead, Covid dead: the mounting numbers should increase our sense of loss and urgency. Instead they numb. Most everyone can empathise with a single bereavement. You understand, I'm sure, why I'm in pain, why my mother hurts; you can imagine what those two young princes, trailing Diana's cortege, might have felt, no matter how distant their life experience is from yours. Yet the woman in Syria or Iraq who loses her entire family, every generation, to a bombing raid – how shall we comprehend her grief? Does she feel each loss as distinct from the other, recognise variations in the degree or manner of her sorrow for every loved one, or is her grief formed like choux pastry, layer upon layer?

I recently joined a private Facebook group, Covid-19 Bereaved Families for Justice UK. I'm not sure I belong, but that's a story for later. The group aims to connect those who have lost someone to Covid and to build momentum for a public inquiry into the government failings that its founders and members hold responsible for at least some of those deaths. As I scroll through the posts, I am struck anew at the unthinking extravagance of our farewell to Andy. I don't mean the cost of Conway Hall or the scale of the event. The whole thing came in below the average cost of a UK funeral, including venue hire and technical support for the films and live music. The biggest bills are for drinks, in Conway Hall after the memorial and then at a local pub we take over, rechristening it, for one night only, the Andy Gill Arms. Old friends make a pub sign for the occasion and also decorate the hall. Friends so new they haven't met Andy create an extraordinary order of service for him, fashioned into the appearance of the sleeve of a vinyl single called 'Kissing You Goodbye'.

The extravagance resides in the opportunity to do just that, to kiss Andy goodbye on his deathbed and again at the funeral and the memorial. There were no restrictions at the hospital except to the numbers allowed next to his bed and even then the nurses bent the rules. There were no limits to the nature or size of his memorial. There was no pressure to assert the tragedy of Andy's death or, so recently, John's, against an unfathomable sea swell of death.

The families in the Facebook group have been deprived of all of these things, barred from bedsides, banned from last moments and limited in the ways they could memorialise. These are losses too great to conjure even or especially in the freshness of my own grief. What happened to them is unimaginable, unacceptable, and still they must fight, not just for justice but to insist on the humanity of those who died. On the Facebook page they tell their stories, honour their dead in the telling, give names and faces to the tragedy.

On the morning of Andy's memorial, Emma and I stand in the kitchen with a large ceramic flagon and a funnel. We're decanting Andy from his cardboard box into the flagon so he can attend his own celebration in suitable attire. As I remove the brown paper liner from the box holding Andy, Emma and I realise too late that it has a hole in it. Some Andy spills onto the counter. We lose more of him into the air during the transfer. When I tell people that Andy is present in every corner of our flat, I doubt they realise quite how literally this is meant.

Most of him lives, still in the flagon, on a high shelf, over-looking my favourite place to sit and read. At first, I spoke to the flagon, without fail, morning and evening. Now I more often talk to my screensaver, a picture I took of Andy on an Italian tour. He stands before a faded, pink stucco wall that has been embellished with the word *CUNT* in several different designs. An ambiguity of angle and expression means that sometimes Andy looks amused, at other times irritated. A portrait made by Shepard Fairey in memoriam now hangs above the staircase. I talk to that too, but mostly I find myself apologising. The artwork is stunning, Andy's expression unmistakably fierce. It's his stage face, his photo face, the pose that earned his band a nickname: Gang of Dour.

For his memorial I am determined to show all of his faces, including the silly ones, the sweet ones, and I am aided in this enterprise by Lise and by Andy's closest friends. He has chosen well if he wished to be memorialised well: the people who love him possess invaluable skillsets for the job in hand, film makers, writers, artists, musicians, sound experts, managers and organisers. We set up WhatsApp groups, begin working on a running order and logistics. The band thinks about how to navigate the gaping absence at their heart.

The solution they come up with breaks me. All day I run back and forth between the flat and the hall with items needed for the memorial – Andy himself, orders of service, scripts, two plastic pigs that I will mention in my eulogy. It isn't until just before we start that I see it, Andy's Stratocaster, on its stand, as if, when the band plays, he might join them.

Somehow I get through the rest of the service. We all do. It is beautiful and painful and perfect. Then the remaining Gang walk on stage, John and Thomas and Tobias. They're all nervous about speaking in public as Andy would have been. Funny how you can perform to thousands but fear speaking to a few hundred. Their tributes are lovely. The song, 'The Dying Rays', breaks me all over again. Everyone is weeping. Everyone is remembering Andy, what he meant to them, what he means.

What will survive of us is love.

Anne's eulogy for John

After more than forty years together, I have just lost the love of my life. Our meeting in 1975 was improbable; in Manchester's newly opened wine bar, I could not get served on a busy Friday lunchtime. I worked for the Arts Council and had parked a very important lady from the National Theatre at a lonely table, to which I had hoped to return speedily. When I unintentionally said out loud, 'How does someone get a drink in this place?' a kind gentleman standing nearby rapidly supplied me with two glasses of white wine and refused to let me pay for them.

He was John Bird and on the surface we may not have seemed a natural fit, coming from different continents and very different backgrounds. He worked in insurance and financial services, I in the arts. And we were both married with children and seemingly secure middle-class lives.

But we were powerfully drawn to each other and found ourselves to be incapable of seeing a future without each other. When I was offered a job as a founder staff member of Opera North in Leeds, we moved there together in 1978 and married in 1980. If John had only been able to hold on until the end of this year, we would have celebrated our fortieth wedding anniversary.

But those are just statistics. What we were, and will always be in my mind, are the two remaining pieces of that difficult jigsaw puzzle which just fit. One can say conventional things such as 'we were close' but we were interlocked. His death has left me emotionally dismembered. But I am sustained by memories of an inseparable relationship with a man who was amazing in so many ways, not least because he loved and totally accepted me for the person I am. He was intelligent, kind, caring, curious, catholic in his tastes and interests and utterly interested in other people. He was also artistic, musical, sporty and a truly wonderful cook, who adored entertaining. He embraced life in every way.

RIP my darling.

Catherine's eulogy for Andy

When Andy loves something, he really loves it. I speak about him in the present tense not because I am in denial – he is dead, I held his hand and stroked his forehead and traced that magnificent dimpled chin as he died. I wept as friends and family spontaneously applauded him at the moment of exit.

I speak about him in the present tense because he endures in this room and far beyond it, in his extraordinary legacy of lives and music transformed by him for the better. He is wonderfully present in the flat we share, in endless funny and poignant reminders, the tape markings on the floor where he practises his kung fu moves, the drumsticks he painstakingly affixed to MDF bases not, as people tend to assume, to create paper towel holders, but to suspend wine carafes to drain after rinsing them. He leaves notes all over the place to himself and to me. There's one that his long-time friend and collaborator Santi and I have been puzzling over, a list of US place names, mostly on the east coast, and in the middle of it the phrase 'pig milking'. We know that pig-milking refers, in some way, to Santi. In one of those music-studio jokes that starts with a silly exchange and develops into an iterative narrative, Andy cast Santi as a pig farmer and over the years they have gifted each other squeaky plastic pigs and other pig memorabilia. Still, we have no idea what the note means. Another note, left in the kitchen for me, is easier to interpret: a heart with an arrow through it and the initials A and C.

My extraordinary good fortune is that Andy loves me and when he loves, he really loves. Unlike some people, love is not, for Andy, a force that focuses on the object of his love to the exclusion of others. His love is expansive. He really loves my family as well as his own. My sisters are his sisters. My parents and step-parents and stepsisters and cousins and godchildren and elective family are a huge part of his life and he of theirs. I will never forget the time my mother sent us an invitation to a significant birthday of hers. She accidentally let slip the position Andy holds in her heart and my family by addressing the envelope to 'Andy Gill plus one'. He really loves his friends, many of whom are here today.

He really loves life and living well. He loves art, music, good design, good food and he loves dogs, though as some of you will know, we have not yet decided which dog to get for ourselves, despite debating this for many years and constantly sending each other pictures of dogs we think may fit our peculiar requirements. You see, we live in central London in a flat with no garden and, even so, Andy is set on a larger dog, which means we need to identify a breed that can flourish in an urban environment. This should be possible, but Andy's slightly odder obsessions complicate the task. He cares a great deal about the ratio between body size and leg length – he can't abide a short-legged dog. And he thinks dogs shouldn't flaunt their arseholes. He is determined that our dog should have a tail that decently covers its arse. Whenever possible we have walked together every Saturday and Sunday afternoon for several hours for most of our lives together and many of our walks are punctuated by Andy exclaiming indignantly over a dog that is showing him its arse.

Ten years ago in Italy, his love for good design, great food and dogs – a particular dog, my sister Lise's dog Biba – collided. We were staying at her hilltop house on our own, enjoying tranquil days of hiking and writing – I a book, he an album. Many mornings he would leave me tapping away at my keyboard to drive down from the hamlet into the local village in search of *bomboloni alla crema*, freshly made doughnuts filled with custard. On this particular morning, he put on his latest acquisition, a fawn-coloured raincoat purchased from the nearby Prada outlet shop, and set off in the car with Biba in the backseat for company. Sometime later I heard him shouting my name, clearly in distress. I ran outside to find him, his raincoat and the hire car liberally decorated in brown puddles and spatters. Biba had suddenly evacuated her bowels over the backseat and then, when Andy turned to look at her, she leapt into his lap and in a final flourish, projectile vomited over the windscreen. I cleaned up everything as best I could – Andy, dog, car, coat – but Biba continued to get sicker. The local vet explained that Biba had probably eaten poison left for foxes; he administered half of a giant syringe of antidote and told us to give her the second half later that night.

When the time came to do this, Andy asked me to hold Biba, readied the syringe, prepared to insert it into the loose skin on her neck, then flinched at the final second – and plunged the needle straight into his thumb. Once I stopped laughing, I retrieved the syringe, gave Biba her injection and tried to comfort Andy, but he was less worried by the pain than the fear of contagion. The next morning, he rang our doctors' surgery in London for emergency advice. He recounted the entire sequence of events, then paused in expectation of a sober, clinical response. I could clearly hear peals of laughter as the doctor, who knew Andy well, failed to restrain her mirth.

Andy makes people laugh, mostly on purpose. He even cracked us up in hospital, as he lay waiting for admission to intensive care, in sepsis and with pneumonia, struggling to breathe. A nurse asked him if he had coughed anything up. Yes, he said. What colour was it?, the nurse asked. Andy looked straight at my sister and me and answered: 'purple'. He knew we would appreciate the joke. When Andy loves, he really loves, and when he conceives dislikes, they are implacable. He dislikes three things even more than an exposed arsehole on a dog: the colour purple, except in some cases in nature, and the texture of velvet and corduroy.

Purple velvet and corduroy both occupy high positions in his pantheon of dislikes. So too do some situations and people, mostly deservedly so, but I don't want in celebrating Andy to construct a hagiography. He is complex and can be grumpy; he's a perfectionist – which is both impressive and sometimes exhausting – and he can turn even the smallest decision, such as where to go to dinner, into a week-long process of philosophical inquiry. When he was in a medically induced coma, one of his many visitors remarked, fondly, that it was the first time they hadn't argued.

Andy also has an idiosyncratic approach to problem-solving. Once, when I joined Gang of Four on tour in Tokyo, he tried to make space in the hotel minibar for a bottle of sake he had been given by the Japanese promoter. Only after removing some of the pre-stocked contents did he realise that this was a minibar that automatically charged the room for each item. I had fallen asleep, jetlagged, and woke as a drink can thudded onto the bed. He'd decided that if he took everything out of the minibar and then replaced it all, the hotel would think the minibar had malfunctioned and cancel the charges. He racked up about a thousand pounds to our bill before he realised this wouldn't work.

The next morning I put all the unopened drinks into a laundry bag, took them to the front desk and persuaded the hotel to waive the charges. It wasn't the first time I'd got him out of a jam and it won't be the last. He has left me with work to complete and tangles to unwind. I know that to the outer world, this looks like a classic gender split – the alpha male, strutting his stuff, enabled by a sensible woman. There's a small extent to which this applies. Many people here will know how difficult it is to get Andy to an airport on time. Early in our relationship, I persuaded him against his better judgement to turn up for our flight the suggested hour before departure. The plane was subsequently delayed and, as we sat in the bar at Gatwick, he drew up a contract for me on a napkin and asked me to sign it. It read 'Everything is always my fault'.

Even so and in many ways, our relationship – our love – endures because he is at least as supportive of me as I of him. I think about the conversation we had, when I told him that the financial risk I was taking in pursuing a lawsuit against TIME magazine might result in us losing our home. 'Fuck them,' he said and meant it. If we had been forced to sell our flat, he would never have reproached me or let me reproach myself.

I think about the nights he's held me as I grieved for people we lost. I think about how well he knows me and how quickly he sees when I'm out of sorts and how often he is able to cheer me up just by pulling one of his silly faces or cooking me a lovely meal. I think how invaluable he is as a sounding board, how clever, how perceptive. I think how fervently he backs the causes that I live and breathe.

I think about the fact that right from the moment we met, he has always made me feel safe in his love. He has never played games. He let me know he wanted to be with me and has never given me cause to doubt that, no matter that we hit bumps in the road, as any couple does.

Andy's love frees up, rather than tying down. Our love for each other means we can look outwards, devote energies to our passions and projects, maintain our connection no matter how far flung his tours or my research trips.

He's further away now than ever before, and I'm not quite sure how this is going to work, but I know that it will. Because when Andy loves, he really loves.

The third letter to John

17 May 2020

Dear John,

Please do not take one word of this letter as criticism, but as a further celebration of your life and our life together. Going through your cluttered and disorganised personal belongings in your cupboards and drawers, your desk and, most recently, your filing cabinet (which collapsed last weekend) has introduced me to a person I realise that I only partly knew. You loved tidiness and organisation; qualities you openly admired in me. As I have already said, the messiness in your final years – clothes not hung up, papers scattered about – was linked to illness. But your secret disorganisation – and some hidden interests – came to light in the drawers of your desk and wardrobe and in your astonishing filing cabinet. Those four drawers could write your biography.

I spent forty-three years nudging and chiding and trying to knock you into shape – my shape. As you know all too well, I am miserly and cautious and excessively tidy and fear above all else things getting out of control. How we managed to get on so well for so long, goodness only knows.

Because through those drawers and files, I have suddenly learned to love and accept the full John Bird, exactly as you were – and I miss you even more. You were romantic, extravagant, fearless, a real chancer not afraid to gamble. You loved and collected everything, and you never, ever bought one of anything. We have the stamp collections, the coin collections, the half-filled photograph albums, the closet full of photography equipment, enough art books and supplies to keep an entire art college going, music in every type of recording piled to the heavens, sheet music for your piano lessons, fine wine, luxury chocolates which I cannot seem to stop from arriving even in lockdown. I think we found about ten wristwatches in your desk, and this after you gave your Swiss watch to grandson Tom and another to grandson Isaac.

No one could have stopped you buying that motorised scooter, which you used about six times. Plants, seeds and gardening supplies are here in abundance; I do not garden, and our gardening service brings their own gear.

Your financial affairs, being slowly unpicked during probate, were just the same. A little nest egg here and there and there again, like a treasure hunt, but sadly not amounting to much when all is counted up. You were comfortable but not rich, yet you lived like a prince. And I say this with nothing less than admiration as I cannot stop worrying for my financial future, especially given the current turbulence, and am already sorting out all my loose ends in case coronavirus carries me away.

One whole filing cabinet drawer was full of your spell as a racing betting tyro, another of your bets on various currencies going up or down, and another of our joint enterprise, Gorgeous Bird, selling Native American jewellery. Behind the racing tips was a fragile paper envelope, which immediately burst open, spilling dozens of Victorian coins, some valuable. Did you even remember it was there? I had to give a bag full of similar things to Ian, because in your desk I found things I could not even identify much less value. I am currently being asked by probate to describe your 'chattels' and their worth. Other than the scooter, not much.

I never met your mother, long dead of cancer when we got together, but frequently spent time with your dad. How he could have sired such a son remains a total mystery. He appeared terrified of anything unfamiliar and discouraged you from following your dreams. He stayed in his army-issue house and seemed uninterested in the world beyond. You were adventurous and brave and never afraid of taking a risk if you thought it was justified. In that respect, you and I were very different. I could never shake the fear that we might go bankrupt. I suppose it goes back to my childhood when my father's death left my mother overnight without any security. You promised me when we first moved to London that the bailiffs would never be at the door and they never were.

You, my darling, lived your nearly 84 years to the full.

Nothing exemplifies your derring-do more than your decision to marry me when you had only just met me, a woman literally from another planet (well, almost literally). It was not just because you fancied me but because I held the key to the door leading to life as you wanted to live it, and the more I plough through the mess you left behind, the more I know I helped you do that, even while not being similar in nature or entirely understanding you.

My favourite two photos of you sit on my desk. One is you at 17 breasting the tape as you win a race with admiring schoolboys and the spire of Salisbury Cathedral in the background. You are tall and thin and look as if you are in the throes of ecstasy, so excited are you to be winning that race. The other is of you as an elderly man, resplendent in your black tie and polished shoes, sitting on a bench in the gardens at the summer opera festival, Glyndebourne. I cannot remember what opera we were seeing that day, but I had as ever taken the opportunity at intermission to go to the loo and was probably at the end of a long queue. You are alone, pensive, holding a glass of champagne, and although you are not smiling you are in the heights of pleasure. You are sitting there thinking 'this is what I want and who I want to be', a very long way from your dad's little army house in Lark Hill.

Though you moved away from your roots, mentally and geographically, you never became snobbish, nor did you take your lifestyle and privileges, all earned, for granted. I was so fortunate to be your other half. Clearing up the messy drawers is a small price to pay.

On 1 May, we were supposed to bury your ashes next to the East Door of your beloved Salisbury Cathedral, as you requested in your end of life notes. That did not happen because of lockdown. But it might have been a blessing in disguise as the weather yesterday was unpredictable and pretty foul – a few sunny intervals interrupted by massive downpours, often with hail, and both windy and fairly cold for May.

I am surprised to say that I rather like having your ashes here with me. I talk to them/you a lot. I had no idea ashes are so heavy and bulky; I had always imagined them as silky and light. Lise went with Catherine to the funeral director to help her collect yours and Andy's because the two sets would have been too much for one person to carry. Apparently Lise took you into a Pret a Manger on the way back to Catherine's. You were in a shopping bag, so none of the customers would have realised. But those ashes, as was true of you, are quite a presence.

I usually don't really listen to the BBC Sunday Service but last weekend I not only listened but wept copiously through most of it. The programme celebrated 800 years since the first foundation stone was laid for Salisbury Cathedral in its current location. Of course there wasn't a congregation as cathedrals are closed alongside theatres and other places where people gather. The service was led by Anna Macham, the precentor, with whom I have exchanged many emails and who has been so helpful in arranging the burial of your ashes. Of course, I now realise that if coronavirus had not intervened, you would have been buried on the very anniversary of the laying of that stone, which must be why your school Bishop Wordsworth holds its Founders Day on the same date. It is named for the Bishop of Salisbury who established it. As Anna and others talked about the cathedral, its spire, its site in the water meadows, Gainsborough's paintings and Salisbury, the tears were coursing down my cheeks. I felt inconsolable as I said the Lord's Prayer with Anna. We will bury you there, my love, I just don't know when.

We are now starting week six of being locked away. Horrible rumours abound about the fate and future of older people. I can assure you that you did well to escape all this, especially as an older person with medical problems. As I told you, the wonderful treatment you received would not have been forthcoming, even at the hospital you loved and served.

I am more fortunate although probate is not proving easy. And of course I am back to worrying about being forced to sell the house. Having told you many times that if you died, I would want/need to move, the opposite is true. I find such comfort in being here. You are in every room with me.

Though I am doing well, my arthritis is very bad indeed and any kind of attention or relief awaits the end of lockdown. The end will be phased and gradual so even if some people can move about in mid-May, it will be at least the end of June until I get out. I have got very angry and political about the way older people are being treated. I offload a lot of my anger in the blogs I am writing for Carole's website.

In one of them I criticised Boris Johnson. He not only survived the virus but has just become a father for at least the sixth time with a new son called Wilfred. Public anger at his muddle and mess as a leader is being somewhat mitigated by sympathy. No one realised, when he was critically ill, that his baby was due so soon. I doubt that sympathy will last. Keir

Starmer has been elected as Leader of the Labour Party; a good choice, although my eldest daughters, both supporters of Jeremy Corbyn as you know, might not agree.

The girls are all fine (although I haven't seen Catherine A in weeks) and George seems also to be surviving life in a nursing home. Grandchildren are well too. Our Friday night family dinners on Zoom continue.

I am working with friend Joanie on my end of life plan as I want things to be easy for the girls. When I saw on Joanie's form, the question about going into a nursing home if I became incapacitated, I could only react with horror. You and I remember the period after the Second World War, when the truth about the death camps began to emerge; there had been mass extermination, millions murdered and many others dying for the lack of food and medical attention. Obviously what's happening now isn't deliberate, industrialised killing, or on anything resembling that scale, but at my age, it carries echoes. Nothing is being done to protect people in care homes from coronavirus and the death tolls are mounting. Until very recently the dead in care homes were not even mentioned or counted in the coronavirus briefings from government. It was as if they weren't human, weren't individuals who had worked hard and paid their taxes and still had people who loved them, but were just old people clagging up the works. So, I am afraid no care home for me, whatever happens.

That means I need to ensure a way to stay here until I die or find another solution. In the short term, I need to keep working out how to live in our house without you. I wish I knew what to do with your studio. It sits there proudly as a sort of museum to you with your work in progress still on the easel and all your paints on the table ready to use. If I had a scrap of talent I would try to paint but I don't. If I do sell the house eventually it will be an asset but for now it is just a painful reminder of things which did not go to plan.

The final reason I started to write this letter is that May has always been my favourite month. I made it through January and February and March and April without you but the thought of completing May without you by my side is so heart-rending that I almost cannot bear it. May for me was the month of hope; the world waking up and bursting into bloom. There seems so little to hope for now, but I will continue to do my best to make you proud of me. And I promise to keep in touch through these letters.

Love,
Anne

Chapter 6: Sadmin

In her own way, the widow loved her husband. Catharine looks at herself in the mirror, studies her face. How is it that the world can tilt on its axis and she appears unchanged? She walks through to the bedroom, lies on her side of the bed. Realises there is no more 'her side'. Rolls into the middle. The tears come.

Long before *Killing Eve*, another story of a ruthless female assassin pursued by a female government agent gains global audiences. The 1987 movie *Black Widow* takes more than three million dollars at the box office in its opening weekend. Reviews are mixed. Critics praise the acting, but pick apart the plot. The tale lacks credibility.

It does indeed, yet the critics miss its largest flaw. Catharine's game is to get rich quickly. She marries wealthy men, then, after two months of feigned marital bliss, spikes their bedtime drinks with poisons that mimic natural causes. If not for the agent who spots a pattern in the deaths, she would be home and dry. After all, she leaves no trail. As soon as her latest husband is cold, she takes control of his assets, liquidates them and vanishes.

Blimey, Catharine. I'd like to meet your probate lawyer.

This is all I can think when, thirty-three years after its release, I sit down to watch the film. I've downloaded pretty much anything I can find with the word 'widow' in the title, on the hunt for clues about my new state. I don't know many widows. My grandmothers eschewed outward signs of mourning, never speaking of this odd, discombobulating condition. They engaged vigorously, travelled widely, wore jeans and primary colours. Hollywood, with its images of black-clad mourners and pale loitering, suggests there may be showier ways to do grief, but I own neither the obligatory veiled hat nor the long gloves. My mother somehow remains immaculate even in lockdown; I change every morning from pyjamas into something resembling pyjamas. I do wear mascara, not to add glamour, but as a deterrent against crying.

If guidance on how to act the part is hard to find, there seems to be no shortage of material telling us how to feel it. A psychiatrist called Elisabeth Kübler-Ross attempted in her famous 1969 book *On Death and Dying* to systematise the stages of grief she had observed in terminally ill patients and their families: these were, she said, denial, anger, bargaining, depression and acceptance. Unable to match my whirling emotions to this roadmap, I wonder if I'm failing to grieve properly. Not that Kübler-Ross intended to prescribe behaviours. In subsequent work, she did her best to puncture the idea that her five stages were sequential or inevitable; she had 'never meant to help tuck messy emotions into neat packages', but the concept had already lodged in public consciousness. A quick Google search of 'stages of grief' turns up multiple representations and variants of Kübler-Ross's list, including a diagram to show how *Avengers Endgame* characters embody each phase. You'll also find charts from an opinion poll surveying members of different UK political parties on the 'five stages of Brexit grief'.

A later chapter of this book touches on the teachings of

psychologists and self-help gurus as distinct from a more personal kind of expertise: lived experience. Here's something my mother and I, living the grief experience as novice widows, could have told you from day one. The bereaved rarely enjoy the luxury of time to explore feelings, in whatever shape or sequence they manifest. Within hours of a death, sometimes even minutes, the newly grieving are confronted with the bureaucracy of death, forms to sign, decisions to take. And so it will continue, months if not years when the five stages of grief jostle for space with Sadmin's seven serfs: Baffled, Lost Docs, Dopey, Grumpy, Sloppy, Weepy and Nothing's Easy.

So condolences, Catharine, but your murderous spree is doomed to failure. Watching *Black Widow* as a widow the improbability of the premise has me shouting at the screen. The simplest Last Will and Testament tangles us in dread tape for an average of 9 to 12 months in England and Wales and it's not so different in America, despite slight variations between states. Once a Grant of Probate has been issued – confirmation that the executor is legally entitled to administer the estate – the heirs should expect to wait at least 3 to 6 months for the disbursement. At time of writing this chapter, seven months since Andy died and with everything slowed by the pandemic, I have yet to get access to his bank accounts, much less sort out the complicated stuff. Unwinding the big fortunes the Black Widow targets is a matter of years, not months. A realistic rewrite would see her spend most of the movie completing forms, calling bereavement lines and still struggling to take possession of her first victim's worldly goods as the credits roll.

Consider the famous real-life case of Anna Nicole Smith. Aged 26, she married an 89-year-old oil tycoon. Photographs of the happy pair, who met in the strip joint that employed her, resemble a still from a version of *Some Like It Hot* in which Marilyn Monroe, not Jack Lemmon, ends up with Osgood. Any comedy swiftly curdled. Smith's husband died after a year, omitting to write his new bride into his Will. She challenged his beneficiaries for a share of the estate. After eleven years, the battle wound its way to the Supreme Court, which ruled in her favour, but she never saw the money. Legal skirmishes continued long after her death from a drugs overdose. A full sixteen years after the first reading of the Will, the presiding judge vented his frustration at the warring parties. 'I am not going to spend a lot of time cutting at nits and gnats for people that are fighting over twenty billion, ten billion dollars that they didn't earn,' he said. 'They didn't create this wealth. It was created by a third party, and they're just fighting over it. They can't agree on anything. They can pay lots of lawyers. They can pay lawyers until hell freezes over. But they don't want to agree to anything. They just want to pay lawyers.' He recused himself from the case.

How many times have my mother and I wished we could recuse ourselves from our own legal and bureaucratic processes? For us, as for most people forced to deal with estates and the many smaller nits and gnats of sadmin, the reality is less high-stakes high drama, more quiet slog. There is also fear.

Anxieties about how she would cope without John clouded my mother's ebbing time with him and intensified after his death. 'I feel complete terror,' she confessed, but I already knew that. Her fear was palpable. John foresaw this, injuncting me to look after her and confiding to Catherine A that he expected my mother to move out of the marital home. It would be too much for her. Catherine remembers the conversation thus:

Me: But why does all your stuff need to be moved and
   sorted?
Dad: Because Anne will want to move when I've gone.
Me: Are you sure? Why would she?
Dad: Well she won't be able to manage – she's too short
   to reach the cupboards.

My mother would not have argued with any part of this assess-
ment. She had never lived independently and the division of
household labour that appeared to make sense when they got
together left her vulnerable when John could no longer uphold
his end of the bargain. There are indeed cupboards and shelves
she can't reach, things around the home she doesn't know how
to fix. She relies on the TV for companionship, tiptoeing round
its multiple controls and habit of sulking if she presses the
wrong button. Coaxing it to behave had been John's domain.
Four decades ago, before moving into their first flat, they'd sat
down and allocated tasks according to existing competencies:
she would clean and iron, he would cook, garden and take on
small repairs. He also handled their joint finances, though she
kept a separate bank account for her professional earnings and
dealt with her own tax returns.

Now she questioned her capacity for managing the unwinding of his estate and taking sole responsibility for her financial affairs. Might the press of a wrong button, as with their
capricious TV set, risk cutting off an essential service? Could
an unforced error strip away such security as she had? She
carried childhood memories of the upheaval that followed the
sequential deaths of her father and brother. Nothing was ever
the same again and there had been some rocky years. Across
the world, the loss of their husbands is liable to plunge women

into precarity and Grandma Ruth had been no exception. My mother craved continuity yet no sooner had John died than friends and family, with the best of intentions, started urging her to the course of action John assumed she'd be eager to pursue: moving home. All she knew was that this advice was at best premature. She didn't yet have the slightest idea where she wanted to live (or, on some days, if) and whether she had a choice in the matter. Already there had been an unpleasant shock lurking in the paperwork. A year earlier, she and John had updated their Wills to reflect changes to their circumstances including the death of his eldest daughter. Somehow in the back-and-forth with their lawyers, he hadn't signed the new version. The old one remained in force.

Blindly, my mother sought to assert control, or at least its illusion, by reaching for smaller, more resolvable issues. She would return John's Blue Badge, his disabled parking permit, and claim the points from his supermarket loyalty card. She must get rid of the equipment that had sustained John and now testified to his absence: his wheelchair, his mobility scooter, his oxygen supplies, his nebuliser. She should clear his cupboards, his desk. Why were all these emails clogging his computer? My sisters and I had to intervene to stop her from deleting, wholesale, correspondence that might prove useful for probate or in compiling the list of people and organisations we should notify of his death.

If these impulses complicated her adjustment to life after John, this was as nothing to the pressures ladled on to her by cumbersome bureaucracies. Next of kin or those who have been present for the death or final illness are required to register a death within days. This is, at very least, a two-step process that starts by obtaining from the hospital the medical certificate stating cause of death, then taking it to the registrar together with additional documentation. The government's website specifies that supporting documents should include the deceased's birth certificate, council tax bill, driving licence, marriage or civil partnership certificate, NHS medical card, passport and some proof of address; in practice, not all of these will be needed, but several forms of identification are essential. Pregnant women routinely pack bags well in advance of their due dates, ready to take to hospital the moment waters break. Not everyone has children, but death, like the Black Widow, is a serial killer and comes to us all. Imagine if we kept sadmin kits at the ready. Instead, after John died, we spent hours rootling around for his driving licence, finding it eventually in a place that, like the rest of his filing system, made perfect sense to him but not to anyone else.

At least before Andy's health so sharply declined and in advance of the pandemic that overburdened the bureaucracies of death, my sisters and I were able to help my mother with some of the initial challenges of widowhood. Cassie and Catherine A, named executors in John's unsigned Will, liaised with the lawyers and the customer services teams of the first organisations and companies contacted with news of John's death. On Christmas Eve, Lise stopped by the hospital for the medical certificate. If she could get through the form-filling fast enough, she would run straight to her appointment with the registrar, the last before the office shut for the holiday season. From the registrar she would order several copies of the death certificate, despite the cost, to show to the companies that demand them before agreeing to close or transfer accounts. She would also collect a second, green certificate required to confirm to the funeral service that the body is approved for burial or cremation.

Her plans nearly came adrift when a hospital employee, American on the evidence of her accent, ushered my sister into a room that resembled a small chapel, with illuminated images of mountain ranges in place of stained-glass saints and a box of tissues on the table. Lise realised she was to be offered, unasked and unwanted, bereavement support. As a diversionary tactic, she asked the employee about her background. Soon they were discussing the US, then the country's politics. This had unexpected merit as a form of therapy. The woman declared herself a Trump supporter, briefly distracting Lise from her grief. She excused herself and made it to the registrar just in time.

To the bereaved, help is both essential and problematic. During the forty-one days between my mother's widowhood and my own, I observed this phenomenon as a daughter trying to get things right. Now I understand the dynamics from both sides, as would-be helper and not infrequently cantankerous helpee.

People, most people, are kind. Fewer know how best to help. Those that do are often informed by their own losses. I remember quizzing my friend Chris, whose wife died six years before Andy, about what I might feel and expect. She warned me against assuming a universality to these things, said 'I can only tell you how I reacted'. She looked after me at the hospital, came with me to fetch the medical certificate – the first time I would see Andy's cause of death spelled out, the first time I would navigate a disturbingly intimate conversation about him as a body. His organs are too wrecked to be of use to anyone, they tell me, his cadaver surplus to requirements for medical schools. Chris also collected the death certificates on my behalf. Another friend Dave, a musician-turned-lawyer, sat through multiple, numbing meetings addressing the legal complexities of Andy's estate, my sounding board and trusted adviser. He was, I knew, without any bias but one: a deep love of Andy.

The value of such support is far above rubies, so too the service provided by staff at companies and organisations who go beyond their mandated roles to help the bereaved. In my tussles with the bank, I encountered such an employee. Covid has given in-branch meetings a whiff of the prison visit; after a series of protocols to gain admission, conversations take place through a perspex barrier. The man behind the screen acknowledged the difficult reasons for my presence and worked as fast as he could to minimise any drain on my time. He also offered tea and sympathy. 'Come back whenever you like, even if you just want a chat,' he said. I was tempted. There's a peculiar urge to share pain with strangers, perhaps to lessen the burden on friends and family, themselves grieving and forced to listen, again and again, to unchanging songs of grief. Bereavement turns us all into jilted lovers, obsessively replaying scenes from the affair as if this could change the outcome or at least make the hurt go away. Denial and bargaining. Bargaining and denial. Coming to terms with loss, whether through death or break-ups, is never easy, but in some ways, break-ups are tougher. I cannot argue with the fact of Andy's death. A moribund relationship holds out the false promise of recovery, of a sudden flicker of the eyes, a squeeze of the hand. It offers neither finality, nor exculpation ('there is nothing more you could have done'); neither closure, nor the same degree of external recognition.

Both kinds of grief, all kinds of grief, deserve respect – that is to say, how a grieving person feels has validity in that moment. Too often the response is to challenge them instead, to frame grief as an aberration, a sickness that will pass. You think your heart is broken, we tell the bereaved, but one day, sooner than you think, it will mend. Not so, the broken heart tries brokenly to reply, to wish away grief is to wish away love.

Grief should be regarded as a temporary and disabling condition only in one single, but highly significant respect: nobody in early-stage grief should make life-changing decisions. The Financial Conduct Authority identifies factors that render customers vulnerable: these include recent widowhood and break-ups. When I made an appointment, after Andy's death, to look into a new mortgage, the adviser replied 'Due to the recent loss of your husband I must let you know we will be treating you as a vulnerable client and I would encourage you to attend with a trusted friend/family member.' Dave accompanied me and I was glad of his presence.

The people who urged my mother and me, as new widows, to sell up, move on, did so out of kindness, but were misguided. So, too, the many friends who beseech me to get a puppy, now that I no longer need negotiate with Andy about leg-to-body-length ratios or arse-covering tails. You cannot force the pace at which grief develops or second-guess where it will lead. My mother expected to be scared of living alone. She recoiled when I first came around with John's ashes. She thought she wanted to clear away reminders of her sorrow. These days she is most content in the home she shared with John, surrounded by him, supported by his presence. His ashes remain there, pending a post-pandemic future that will allow us to reinstate the plans to bury them in the grounds of Salisbury Cathedral. She is coping with sadmin too.

My sisters and I are getting better at enabling her to figure out what she wants to do rather than telling her what to do. What helps her most is not instruction but midwifery as she births, in her own time, new strategies and routines for living. One of her first blogs for the over-fifties website lamented her bossy daughters ticking her off for her reluctance to use the technologies that, once lockdown had been imposed, became essentials. We weren't wrong to get her a smartphone, but perhaps we should have guessed that she wouldn't want to proceed straight to ordering meals from Deliveroo. First she had to accustom herself to a touchscreen. She adapted to Zoom more quickly because the platform enables her to hold business meetings – she is still freelancing – as well as joining social events. She does so via Lise's old iPad. I set up Zoom on her computer before realising that her whiskery machine included neither a camera nor speakers.

I ask her if she has any stand-out memories of things and people that have helped her to this point. She doesn't need to reflect for long, immediately singling out 'the lovely man from Wheel Freedom who came to take back John's rented wheelchair and was just so compassionate and understanding and kind. Up there with him, tied for first place, is Pasquale, who will remain part of my life.'

This doesn't surprise me. Watching her with Pasquale, who has been coming around to look after the garden since John could no longer do so, I realised that their discussions about shrubs and flowers are also conversations with and about John. The garden is an expression of my stepfather, something he created and nurtured, my mother its keeper. With Pasquale, she discusses how best to handle this living legacy. It doesn't feel right to preserve it like a petal in amber. John and Cassie loved their annual visits to the Hampton Court Flower Show, returning laden with seeds and the seeds of ideas. My mother enjoyed trailing along with them but never shared their passion. These days she looks at the garden with fresh eyes. Two years ago Pasquale planted an echium by the front door, which quickly reproduced. Already one plant is three times her height. As she stares up, rapt, bees dart among its blossoms and I think of Jack and his giant beanstalk reaching to the clouds. Does she spy John at the distant tip?

I too tend to my love's legacy. Morning, noon and night, something always demands attention, whether a sync request to use Andy's music in a film or TV show, a bill for a vinyl pressing or a legal letter, the good, the expensive and the ugly, endless and unsettling, a leaf drift of memories banked against every song that lawyers discuss as if it were simply a piece of property.

I never aspired to this responsibility. Far from it. To the canon of toxic representations of widows add keepers of the flame, the women who devote their lives to the memory of Great Men, polishing and sanitising until they and the Great Men lose definition – or so their critics allege. T. S. Eliot's second wife, Valerie, took care over editing his letters, attracting for her pains snide comments about censorship. In defending his depiction of George Orwell's widow as a gold-digger, his biographer Michael Shelden declared that she 'found herself confronted with a generous proposal of marriage from a famous novelist with a fatal disease.' He added: 'To pretend that money didn't play a part in her decision is absurd.' Sonia Orwell had told a friend that her husband used his illness to pressurise her into marrying him, but the explanation cut no ice with Sonia's detractors. Natasha Spender, widow of the poet Stephen, faced accusations of covering up his gay relationships; Jill Balcon, after the death of her husband Cecil Day-Lewis, of concealing his straight relationships. 'No weak men in the books at home,' as Gang of Four sang on 'Not Great Men', a track from their debut album *Entertainment!*

The last thing I wanted was to find myself in the position of asserting and defending the last things that Andy wanted. Yet what else was I to do? He omitted to express his last wishes within the formal confines of a Will or any other document that would have lightened the weight of sadmin and devolved at least a few of these responsibilities. He did, however, make his last wishes clear to me and to everyone who saw or spoke to him in those final weeks. He wanted the music he had written and recorded to come out; he wanted the covers album to see the light.

On our return from Italy and as Andy grew weaker, we fixed an appointment for the end of January to draw up our Wills. Our new lawyer, specialising in probate and, crucially, with detailed understanding of the workings of the entertainment industry, came recommended via our friend Dave, who was to act as Andy's executor. We originally agreed to meet the lawyer at his office, but Andy's increasing fragility forced a change of proposed venue, first to our flat, then to the hospital. By the day of the appointment, Andy lay in a coma, scheduled for a withdrawal of life support. After he died, I retained the lawyer for the sadder job of applying for a Grant of Representation, the only course of action open in view of Andy's intestacy.

We jointly owned our flat but had kept our finances largely separate. The Grant of Representation process, just like a probate application, involved compiling and submitting to the court an accurate estimate of Andy's assets and liabilities, no easy task without even a rudimentary list of either and with all the complexities of a music estate. Within weeks and amid the resurgence of a rights dispute stretching back years, I had to retain a second lawyer, a litigation specialist that Andy had consulted. I also hired Andy's former manager Aaron to work with me on future releases and on tending to the back catalogue, took on PR people in the UK and US for those future releases, plus another set of lawyers and experts to sort out the multiple legal agreements needed for the covers album. On top of that, Aaron recommended a new merchandising company and additional freelance help. Around the same time, I suggested to Andy's friend Santi, a musician and sound engineer, that we collaborate on running Andy's home studio. Santi looked at me strangely. 'I was going to raise the same idea,' he said. 'In about six months.' We commissioned building works to prepare the studio for its new incarnation.

So much for not making life-changing decisions in early-stage grief. Meetings bit huge, undigestible chunks out of each day, face-to-face soon giving way to a peasouper of lockdown Zooms, and on each of those days someone, meaning these words kindly, would remark 'It's good to keep busy'.

I'm not looking for sympathy here. I know very well how privileged I have been, as a widow, to worry about degrees of financial security rather than degrees of financial desperation, how lucky to enter the turbulence of pandemic and Brexit with savings and a half-share of a London flat that, at the end of probate, would be entirely mine. My concerns were urgent, but they were never existential. They just felt that way at times. I had no income, no access to estate funds and my outgoings were spiralling. The pandemic raised questions over the viability of all of these plans, paused the building work and knocked out my only prospective fee-paying jobs, as a public speaker. Logic dictated that I should, at very least, put the brakes on some of these projects. I couldn't and didn't. As I say, what else was I to do? When the person you love dies, you're not freed from any compacts you've made but more closely bound to them. Andy could not represent himself. I must act for him and quickly, to timelines dictated by the projects.

The irony wouldn't have escaped Andy. Throughout our years of marriage, I'd done my best to avoid getting embroiled in the music business. From me Andy got, when asked, advice and occasional lyrics; and, more grudgingly, limited logistical support with tours and the studio. This often consisted of dealing with crises created by Andy's approach to packing and punctuality. His tour managers devised strategies to try to corral him into compliance, but always he'd thwart them. I think about the time quite recently that he inveigled our hairdresser into giving him a trim at our flat the morning the band was due to fly to Argentina. Preparations continued around him for their departure to the airport. I kissed him and headed off to see a friend in North London. I always hated goodbyes. About halfway to my destination, my phone rang. He had left an essential inhaler for his sarcoidosis in my bag. I returned home as fast as possible to find the splitter van loaded and ready. They should still make the flight.

As the tour manager messaged me later, they came close to missing it anyway. Andy dropped his passport on the way to the airport, forcing the driver to make the same kind of screeching U-turn I'd performed earlier. Nor did the problems stop there. On arrival in Buenos Aires, Andy realised he'd forgotten to pack any clothes apart from his stage gear. I might have laughed, indulgently, at this news, but for the fact that I'd just removed a load of washing and discovered every item covered in what appeared to be fur. Andy had placed a towel filled with his hair trimmings straight into the machine. 'Doesn't hair dissolve?' he asked, when I complained.

Our relationship sustained because our interests and passions intersected and sparked but remained distinct. Tour managing him would have driven me round the twist. Andy periodically tried to involve me more closely in his work, but recognised the importance of our independence too. 'You encourage each other to thrive in whatever it is that you're trying to do,' Andy told the *Sunday Times*. 'And, you know, she's always liked to have a lot on her plate, a lot of stuff that she has to deal with, and I suppose I do as well. But you try to help each other.'

We'd developed strategies for happy coexistence, but this wasn't the only reason I reacted to the idea of deeper engagement with the music industry like a vampire to a cross. It's not that I don't love music and more than a few of our friends in the industry. At Gang of Four gigs you would always find me in the mosh pit. Why watch Andy from the sidelines when I could be in the thick of it, in the sweet spot between walls of noise, where every sound is crystalline and you feel the beat a fraction before you hear it?

What I shied from was the industry around music. For years, I had staff jobs as a journalist. If I wanted to hang with a crowd with no idea of people management and a habit of staying up all night, I could go to my office. If I craved time around shouty old lechers, I could go to Westminster. And politics and the media appeared paragons of inclusivity and good working practices compared to the music business. Its culture is surprisingly feudal, full of strutting overlords and *droit de seigneur*. It mistakes bad behaviour for creativity and prizes unprofessionalism for the same reason. When the *Sunday Times* asked Andy whether being married to me had given him 'an insight into feminist issues' in music, he demurred. 'Funnily enough not particularly,' he replied, 'because it's always been so screamingly obvious. It's endemic, all through society and the workplace and everything but I was at a Music Producers Guild judging afternoon where we judged different bits of music for various awards, like Producer of the Year, Engineer of the Year, Mixer of the Year, that kind of thing and we're about to start and there's not one woman in this room. There's a hundred men.'

Oh my love, thanks to you, there's now a woman in the room. She doesn't want to be there and she misses you so very much.

One morning, I get a text message. It tells me that FedEx will deliver my parcel shortly and gives me a tracking number. I'm not expecting anything, so assume this is either a sympathy gift or an incoming legal letter. True, people keep sending flowers, but these generally arrive without prior notice. The flat is streaked with pollen, flecked with fallen petals. Each bouquet must be wrestled out of protective layers of such strength and overspecification that it seems as if the florist fears their living wares will make a break for it. You can see why they might. The blooms vibrate with energy. It falls to me to keep them in this condition for as long as possible.

Snip the stems at an angle. Quick, add plant food to the water. Let the new arrivals eat and drink. Arrange them as artfully as you can. Surely you can do better than that! Find a suitable place for them, cool and out of direct sunlight. Talk to them, if you will. It makes a change from talking to the dead. Keep them fed and freshly watered. These are your companions now. Yet, no matter how hard you try, the flowers droop, drop and die. At the end of every week, I clear away their corpses. When I comment on this, a Jewish friend tells me that Judaism shuns floral arrangements as a mark of sympathy, partly because of these unintended resonances and also as distractions from grief that the bereaved will feel better for embracing.

Frankly, how I feel at this point is rough. I haven't been sleeping well. I hardly sleep at all. At least my wakefulness spares me from dreaming. The few dreams that do break through cling to me for hours. One night I smuggle Andy into a hotel in a suitcase. The case feels too light, so I open the catches and find him suffocating. Other dreams are sweet. We sit together, laugh, play table football or, under the dinner table, footsie. These sequences feel more real than real life because, for so much longer than our current reality, that's what they were. To awake to the empty present is to lose Andy all over again.

Still, tonight I am determined to sleep. My GP has prescribed diazepam. I need to be fit to deal with sadmin and all the music-related business. The previous Friday, Valentine's Day and Andy's funeral, we released the single 'The Dying Rays'. Already we are working on a new EP, *ANTI HERO*, and plan to donate proceeds to the NHS charity associated with St Thomas's Hospital.

So, what time will this mystery parcel arrive? I enter the tracking number into the FedEx website. The Fedex virtual assistant tells me the courier should be with me momentarily. The moment comes and goes. All day the assistant issues fresh promises, then reneges on them. By 10 p.m., my virtual tormentor tells me the following: 'Your package is expected to be delivered on Wednesday, 19 February 2020 at 00:00'.

What to do? I'm unable to penetrate FedEx's defences to reach a human being. The assistant refuses to let me reschedule. Eventually I decide to go to bed. I take the diazepam but lie awake all night, listening for the doorbell which never comes. The next morning, the assistant sends me a new delivery time.

When, several days later, the consignment finally arrives, I see it is a small envelope. Oh dear, I think: all the hassle and this is going to be a document I need to sign or a demand I won't like. I open the envelope with trepidation, find another, even smaller, envelope and, inside that, a scrawled, handwritten note: condolences from a rock star.

Holding the note, I laugh out loud. This sums up every well-intentioned gesture gone astray since Andy's death, every reason I love some people in the music industry, including the sender of this note, while shrinking from a culture that sends non-urgent notes by courier and assumes a non-virtual assistant to take delivery.

Ah well. I'd better get used to it.

The fourth letter to John

25 May 2020

Dear John,

How can you not be here? Five months after you died in the cold and grey of late December, we are in glorious late spring/early summer. April and May have been incredibly hot and sunny with almost no rain and very few cool days. The garden is looking so beautiful and I keep imagining you inspecting it in detail and enjoying it so much.

Pasquale cannot speak of you without a tear in his eye. As I mentioned, he could only take care of the front garden because of the savage restrictions of our lockdown. But two weeks ago he and his young assistant Joe went through the neighbour's small granny house (with her permission of course) and climbed the fence with all their equipment including the mower. Now the back garden is really taking shape again. They are back on

Thursday (over the fence) as we all await news of the easing of lockdown. Remember when I first wrote that I said to you with horror that we might be locked up for three weeks!? It is now ten weeks and no end in sight. A very new way of life.

I am trying to take much more interest in what Pasquale and Joe do and we have jointly asked your pardon for letting the gorgeous yellow poppies remain. The roses are magnificent although lack of water is beginning to affect them. The sprinkler goes morning and evening but not at hot midday. Pasquale has been propagating vegetables for the patch. The neglected rhubarb is about six feet high and we are leaving it because we both love the way it looks.

In the front garden the twenty-two-foot echium is attracting tourists and we have featured twice in the local newspaper. A friend took a photo of little me next to it last week, which I have circulated to friends and family. The climbing rose which was our housewarming present from Sarah was also magnificent this year although it is withering a bit. And where the rosebush on the side of the garage seems to have died, Pasquale has planted a Virginia creeper so the wall will be scarlet by autumn 2021. It just seems impossible that you are not here to see and enjoy what you loved so much – your garden.

Indoors I have had good luck with the orchids, most of which have bloomed or are blooming. I still pay a fortune for cut flowers even though for ten weeks, one brief visit a week from Catherine represents the only person other than me to look at them. However, she and I have invited Ian and Jayne to tea in the back garden next Sunday. They will go swiftly through the house without touching anything but we can space out in the garden when we get there.

I'm still worrying about what to do about your studio. Without a regular income you somehow raised quite a lot of money to build a wonderful studio space with small tool shed attached. I fought against it as I thought it would blight the back garden, but it is set sideways and fits right in. No one else can use it because they would have to go through the house and I am anyway not certain I want anybody rearranging it. Catherine A and I have now moved your ashes there, pending any possibility of going to Salisbury with them.

Because of lockdown and isolation, it feels as if everything is frozen and nothing happening. For instance, the car is still in the garage and the wine still to be appraised although I am getting through the white quite nicely. Small pleasures, as you would say.

You would not recognise your country nor your city. With the fine weather and the total fuzziness of the Johnson government, people have taken matters into their own hands and decided the pandemic is all over and they can do what they like. This is the late May bank holiday weekend and our local square looks like Benidorm in high season. Our road has turned into a thoroughfare for pedestrians and cyclists who, deprived of their pubs, just seem to be wandering around. Bullets were fired in the square last Saturday and the police cordoned it off for forty-eight hours but found no culprits or bodies, just a few spent shell casings.

Garden centres have just reopened and the queue for the one around the corner is incredible. People stand patiently in the heat to go in one by one. Estate agents are working again and my fears have returned that Ian and Jayne will sell their house; it feels dreadful wishing them not to when they are so keen to move. The slow relaxation of lockdown means that we can now have a 'bubble' with one other household and they are mine.

People are also allowed to gather in groups of up to six people outdoors and I have been giving some small parties in the back garden, which means that those people have to walk through the house. Our daughters worry that I am taking too many risks, whereas I am just trying to balance widowhood/ solitude with some very modest form of social life. But at least I am aware of and observing the main regulations, such as social distancing, which is not true of many. Whenever I hear praise for the way the general public is behaving under lockdown regulations, I do wonder which general public they mean.

Boris Johnson refuses to give us any sensible guidelines or deadlines and is currently caught up in a huge scandal defending his chief adviser, Dominic Cummings, who took his wife and young child to Durham during the fiercest period of lockdown when we were not allowed to travel or visit elderly parents. What made it worse is that Cummings did this knowing he had coronavirus. Government rules are strict about self-isolating so as not to spread the virus. Cummings seems both obnoxious and arrogant, but Johnson is not prepared to let him go. He (Cummings) held an hour-long press conference at Downing Street today defending what he had done, and Johnson backs him all the way. You would be having so much fun on Facebook dispensing your opinions without fear or caution. As you know, I have never taken an interest in social media but so many people are missing your outspoken opinions on Facebook and in person. You absolutely never minced your words nor would you be doing now.

You would surely have a lot to say about how much the arts are suffering. Performance arts depend on people rehearsing in the same space and then audiences sitting in closely confined auditoria next to people they do not know. The general opinion is that spring 2021 will be our earliest return to live performances, and although the large theatres are experimenting with distanced seating and very reduced audience sizes, the fringe theatres we know and love will be lucky to get back on their feet again, if ever.

On another tack, you would be wryly amused by a piece I just saw in *The Guardian*. Unused and unsold vintage French wines are being converted into hand sanitiser; no one wants wine but there has been a huge scramble for sanitiser, to the extent that it is hard in shops to find anything like mouthwash which contains even a drop of alcohol. The mouthwash my dentist wishes me to use is going for £25 a bottle on Amazon; I used to buy it for £3.50 at Sainsbury's.

In many ways, though, I am coping. The girl who was afraid to be in the house alone and needed you to do so many things is still here but encased in a new and tougher exterior. Ever since they wheeled you away on 2 December with a cheery shout, 'don't worry, he will be home in a few days,' I have had to cope.

I am braver and more competent. Wrestling with probate has taught me a lot about money and finances which I should have known a long time ago. Alongside UK probate, I am trying to sort out my US affairs and leave things in good order for the girls. Both the US and UK have had record numbers of Covid-19 deaths with millions out of work or 'furloughed'. Services in both countries are at a standstill.

The US is in the middle of the worst race riots since the murder of Martin Luther King Jr. back in 1968. A Black man called George Floyd was killed in Minneapolis in broad daylight when a white police officer knelt on his neck, observed by three white colleagues who did nothing to stop him. Floyd gasped 'I can't breathe' repeatedly and then died. The nation and then the world exploded with rage.

Because the world outside is in such turmoil, the unnatural quiet of the house is welcoming. I feel safe here. I am, thank goodness, virus-free and could never have made it through the past months without the help of family and friends and neighbours, most especially Catherine. I am not afraid to ask for help but self-sufficiency is creeping up on me. I have been no further than the high street for twelve weeks, nor used public transport.

I eat a lonely dinner every night, initially geared to listening to *The Archers* so I didn't feel so alone but they ran out of programmes (you cannot gather in a radio recording studio any more than in a theatre rehearsal room). Now I watch whatever the TV has to offer. If it fails to work, which is not infrequent, I cannot shout for John to come and fix it. Ditto the phone, the computer and the burglar alarm.

I am slowly teaching myself not to panic but the hamster wheel which is my brain churns on. My dreams are lurid and active, and you are always in them. I try so hard to hold on to them, but they are soon gone.

So, I am acquiring new skill sets (although I'm not yet polishing shoes or silver – those are still your jobs), and have decided to stay in the house if humanly possible. It seems that I am learning at the age of 86 to stand on my own two feet, polished shoes or not.

Love,
Anne

Chapter 7: Covid

The truth, like grief, can be slippery. A journalist might write a piece that is correct in every laboriously fact-checked detail but, in missing the wider context, misleads. This applies to articles written from perspectives of unconscious bias, the white man who inveighs against 'identity politics' without noticing that he assumes 'white man' to be the default, or the columnist exhorting us to pull ourselves up by our bootstraps without seeing that some sections of the population are denied access to bootstraps. It is also the case for journalism based on information that is partial, by happenstance or design.

Just after John died and into the first months of the implacable new year, such stories were plentiful. Health authorities in Wuhan had flagged up an emerging disease on the last day of December. In early January, China revealed the pathogen to be a novel coronavirus, SARS-CoV-2. It should have been apparent to any government responding to this emerging threat that trusting to herd immunity – building resistance to the contagion within populations by allowing its spread – would be wildly risky. Such immunity comes about only after more than half of a population has been infected or vaccinated and developed defences against the disease. Nobody knew if Covid survivors enjoyed any level of protection or sustained any longer-term damage. Nobody knew if a vaccine could even work.

Most everything about the disease appeared a mystery, from its origins to its methods and ease of transmission to its incubation period, impacts and possible treatments. Many of these questions remain open even now, and every new piece of the puzzle sparks additional questions. The what-ifs swarm like blowflies. What if the virus had come to attention sooner? What if governments had been more transparent? What if scientific advice had been better or better taken? Might lives have been spared? My mother and I are pestered by another buzzing doubt: what killed John and Andy? We thought we knew.

We understood that they had died before Covid-19, not because of it. Then something happened to shake our certainty and send me delving into a news story that had just become intensely personal. This, too, is a function of grief, the drive to establish the facts even when they cannot change the outcome. For some of those bereaved by and during the pandemic, there is another, intertwined impulse – for justice. Populist leaders dismissed the threat of coronavirus while blocking measures to combat it. Governments failed and fumbled. How can you ever reach Kübler-Ross's fifth stage, acceptance, if the people or institutions at least in part responsible for the death of your spouse, your parent or grandparent, aunt or uncle, sibling or cousin, your child, your friend, continue to act with impunity?

What pushed me to investigate was something else again: if Covid had played a role in John and Andy's deaths, that would prove that the virus reached Europe significantly earlier than the official version of events allowed; that its path and patterns stood at odds with current thinking. It would mean that the public health response in the UK and elsewhere was based on flawed data and urgently needed to be recalibrated. In seeking to establish what happened to John and Andy, I now realise that I was trying to contain the spread of grief.

At the beginning of lockdown, before Jo sent me the map of historic London trees, my daily walks retraced a different history. They took me to Andy's old flat in Mile End, to our first home together, near Tower Bridge, and followed our favourite routes, to Borough Market, Tate Modern, St Paul's, or westwards to Soho, Marylebone, Regent's Park and the Serpentine. Absence recast each familiar vista, emptiness reflected in windows and puddles and the sluggish brown of the Thames. I began to take photographs mirroring pictures from earlier walks, identical but for the missing person at the centre of the frame. I posted these before-and-after pairs on social media under the title *Landscapes with and without Andy*.

When I ran out of destinations within easy walking distance, I walked further, twelve kilometres, fifteen, day in, day out. My feet hurt, my toenails blackened, but I needed to express the grief of irretrievable loss. Nothing could ever be the same. This wasn't only true of my small life. Central London lay deserted, a ghost town, boarded up and bleak, more foxes than people, more rats than foxes.

Stickers were proliferating, too, on lampposts and junction boxes. 'Open your eyes,' they proclaimed. 'It's a con. Chemtrails, vaccines, 5G will kill you.' A quick internet search revealed variants of the conspiracy theory behind this strange message. Coronavirus had been engineered by state actors or multinationals seeking to cover the damage to populations caused by radiation from wireless cellular networks, especially the newest technical standard, 5G. A more elaborate version linked 5G to a Chinese or international plot. 'The Chinese were all given mandatory vaccines last fall,' read one of many similar – and similarly off-the-wall – posts. 'The vaccine contained replicating, DIGITISED (controllable) RNA which were activated by 60Ghz mm 5G waves that were just turned on in Wuhan (as well as all other Countries using 60Ghz 5G) with the "smart dust" that everyone on the globe has been inhaling through chemtrails. That's why when they say someone is "cured", the "virus" can be "digitally" reactivated at any time and the person can literally drop dead.'

Conspiracy theories, like stopped clocks, are sometimes right for the wrong reasons. Area 51, in the Nevada desert, deserves its longstanding reputation as the locus for unidentified flying objects, but confirmation in 2013 that it is a secret United States Air Force facility underscored the strong probability that the lights seen streaking across American skies were experimental aircraft or test missiles rather than visiting aliens. Obvious explanations are, more often than not, the right ones, yet ours is a world grown suspicious of the authorities and institutions who provide the explanations. In 2019, more than two thousand people, at least some clinging to their own truths, converged on the site, inspired by a Facebook page called 'Storm Area 51, They Can't Stop All of Us'.

The 5G theory has been debunked, again and again, only to be revived, again and again. *The authorities and institutions insist this isn't true, therefore it must be true.* The logic of conspiracists is an unbreakable loop. After a series of arson attacks on mobile phone masts a month into lockdown, Professor Stephen Powis, the National Medical Director of NHS England, begged for public understanding that the 5G network was not only innocent of responsibility for the pandemic but essential to combating it. 'I'm absolutely outraged and disgusted that people would be taking action against the infrastructure we need to tackle this emergency,' he said.

There was, as it happened, at least one 5G conspiracy. The news agency Reuters obtained an internal European Union document, dated 16 March. 'A significant disinformation campaign by Russian state media and pro-Kremlin outlets regarding Covid-19 is ongoing,' it said. 'The overarching aim of Kremlin disinformation is to aggravate the public health crisis in Western countries... in line with the Kremlin's broader strategy of attempting to subvert European societies.' Russian trolls and bots had helped to disseminate the myths about 5G. Just because you're paranoid doesn't mean that someone isn't out to get you – and we aren't wrong to be suspicious of authorities and institutions. The problem is that our loss of trust instead of proofing us against lies and untruths is making us more vulnerable to them.

For most of my working life, I've observed, with fascination and concern, a precipitous decline in confidence in church, state, politics, media and the other bodies and structures that shape and communicate attitudes; I've tried to understand the causes and myriad effects. In my book *Amortality*, I explored the ways in which this fracturing had altered our expectations of ageing and death. Later I was drawn to write a biography of Prince Charles and to examine his influence on different areas of life because opinion polls showed Britons trusted the unelected royal family far more than elected officials, far more than many kinds of experts, and this despite a series of crises, scandals and, in 1997, the death of his former wife Diana.

The poll findings were counterintuitive. Two years after the crash in the Pont de l'Alma tunnel, investigating magistrates in France had handed down their judgment: the intoxication of the driver, Henri Paul, was a key cause of the crash. The magistrates criticised photographers for giving high-speed chase and clustering at the scene, but ruled there was no criminal case to answer. Their decision did nothing to convince those who believed in dark conspiracies, cleaving to their own elaborate versions of events in an attempt to make sense of the senseless, the unpredictable circumstances that placed a princess in the back of a speeding vehicle, a comet's tail of paparazzi streaming behind her.

How could Paul's parents grieve in peace while their son shouldered so much blame? The magistrates made a point, in their judgment, of offering mitigation; he had not expected to be on duty that night. This was not enough to spare him a post-mortem monstering in global media. His parents came to suspect he must be the innocent victim of a plot against Diana and her lover Dodi, eventually launching a civil suit in an attempt to prove the blood samples showing drugs and alcohol in Paul's body had been taken from another corpse. Dodi's father, Mohamed Al-Fayed, pursued alternative theories for the crash with the single-mindedness that paparazzi had shown on the night, blaming them, the royal family, the security services – anyone and anything but bad luck.

I always had sympathy for these manifestations of grief while seeing in the huge, exploitative industry of sensationalist media that grew up around the events of that night, the merchandising and monetising of suspicion, not just the darker side of humanity but symptoms of a clear and present danger. There had always been conspiracy theories, but the internet gave them wings and turbocharged the crisis in public trust. Journalism, deprived by the digital revolution of the economic models that sustained it, struggled for survival, often to the detriment of quality and principle, validating cynicism about mainstream journalism just when a strong independent press was most needed, with populist politics rushing into the vacuum created by the weakness of the political mainstream. The surging populists deliberately sowed mistrust of any person or institution that could challenge their demagoguery, attacking journalists and judiciary, piling lie upon lie. Old politics responded by becoming more populist. Data technologies that might have shown us the world more clearly instead polarised and microtargeted voters in democratic societies, surveilled and suppressed the citizens of totalitarian regimes.

These days misinformation spreads like a virus; we believe everything and nothing. The coronavirus pandemic would have been a tragedy whenever it hit, but its timing and context made it deadlier.

My love died on Brexit day. This is incidental and coincidental, but it speaks to that wider context.

His rapid deterioration had surprised the doctors looking after him. He was comparatively young, comparatively fit. They had been able to identify a fungus in his sarcoid-damaged lungs and tailor treatment to target these two conditions. You'll be out of here in no time, they said. They were right. His breathing worsened, his oxygen levels dropped, his other organs began to fail. Nobody could come up with a definitive reason, but staff who work in intensive care units are used to the luck of the draw. Grieving relatives demand to know exactly why their loved ones die but sometimes no amount of data from machines, laboratories or post-mortems can fully answer their questions.

The void attracts unfortunate theories. The dead are blamed, by implication, for their own deaths: they 'gave up the fight', as if mortality yielded to force of will. Medical staff, too, become the focus of suspicion, on occasion for good reason. Quite a few of the Covid-19 Families for Justice group tell stories of fatal steers by the NHS 111 phone service or of Do Not Resuscitate notices applied with impossible haste. When Cassie's close companion Maurice died, he had been pursuing, for some years, a malpractice claim against a surgeon who during an operation for prostate cancer perforated his bowel and potentially distributed cancer cells more widely throughout his body. The lawsuit lapsed with Maurice's death.

None of this applied to Andy. His treatment was exemplary, attentive, inventive and caring. That it failed seemed inexplicable – nor did I seek an explanation, much less apportion blame. When the conspiracy theories started, I rejected them outright.

How could he have succumbed to Covid-19? The timelines couldn't be reconciled with official information on the spread of the disease, in China or to Europe, or ideas about how quickly it developed. The ground zero cases in Wuhan weren't even logged until late December. The virus supposedly made landfall in England at the end of January; the first British cases were diagnosed on the last day of that month, on the eve of Andy's death. Gang of Four's tour, in November, had taken the band to Beijing, Shanghai and Guangzhou, not to Wuhan. If, despite all of this, Andy had come into contact with a carrier on his trip, he'd surely have shown symptoms shortly after his return to London. Moreover both of us believed, on the basis of a conversation with one of his doctors, that he'd been tested for the new coronavirus and found to be negative.

Later, as images and descriptions of Covid fatalities appeared not as news bulletins but stinging memories, continued questions about Andy's cause of death struck me as prurient at best. Journalists sent messages purporting to condole but configured to pry. When I didn't answer, they followed up. Have you received the email, the letter, the text? Somehow I'd missed the clause in the etiquette of grief injuncting the bereaved to send thank you notes for condolences.

One night I turned on the TV to a report from Italy's intensive care wards, close-ups of patients on ventilators, a voice-over about how they were gasping for breath. How lauded was this report on social media – and how inaccurate. You could see that the patients were in induced comas, as Andy had been, the rise and fall of their poor chests mechanical. I threw up for hours.

Then, in May, a friend sent me a link to a French newspaper. Researchers had found evidence of the virus in samples taken from a man called Amirouche Hammar, a patient hospitalised north of Paris the previous December. The story prompted little interest in the UK, but hit me like a train. I'd been trying to avoid Covid coverage. Now I watched and read everything, papers in scientific and medical journals too, checking my layperson's interpretations with Andy's cousins, a family of scientists including one who had been drafted to work on combating the pandemic. I also struck up a correspondence via Twitter with Nick Gay, an academic at Cambridge University with a long pedigree and extended job title to match: Professor of Molecular and Cellular Biochemistry, Wellcome Trust Senior Investigator.

Nick got in touch because he had known Andy in their student days at Leeds University. His own experience had led him to question Chinese timelines for the emergence of the virus. 'My son and his family were living in Beijing and I travelled out to visit them on 27 December,' he emailed. 'Before I arrived my granddaughter became really quite unwell with a flu-like illness and my son took her to the hospital in Beijing where they did a battery of tests including RT-PCR for flu and other respiratory viruses but found nothing. Fortunately she improved and we were able to follow through with our plan to spend new year in Cambodia. By the time we got back to Beijing my son had developed all the symptoms we would now associate with Covid-19 and it took him several weeks to completely recover. I left Beijing on the 11 January with a similar though milder respiratory tract infection.'

He ended that first email with a quote from Albert Camus' *The Plague*: 'Everybody knows that pestilences have a way of recurring in the world, yet somehow we find it hard to believe in ones that crash down on our heads from a blue sky. There have been as many plagues as wars in history, yet always plagues and wars take people equally by surprise.'

I needed answers. It wasn't just that the accepted Covid timelines had been thrown in doubt. Expectations of Covid-19's incubation period were also in flux. A man in Wuhan had entered lockdown in apparent good health, exhibiting symptoms only after twenty-seven days; other cases pointed to the disease taking anything between days and weeks from infection to outward signs of illness. It seemed that Covid, like grief, was a shape-shifter. Patients might develop a mild flu-like condition, appear to recover, then relapse and decline. In combination, this new data drove a fist through the defences I'd built against speculation about Andy, my own included. I'd last emailed Professor Santis to ask if my love's chances would have been better if I'd got him to hospital sooner. Now I contacted him again. 'Do you think,' I wrote, 'that there's a possibility that Andy was an early victim of Covid-19? I cannot shake that suspicion.'

His reply winded me. 'Your question is one that I asked myself more than six weeks ago,' he replied. 'It seemed to me at the time of Andy's illness that we had not fully understood why he deteriorated as he did. Once we learned more about Covid-19, I thought there was a real possibility that Andy had been infected by SARS-CoV-2. I discussed this with colleagues in early March – I thought we should explore this further once we had the tools to answer the question such as reliable antibody tests. I did not want to contact you until and if I had a definite answer.' He will later add that 'the fresh abnormalities in Andy's lungs were not typical of what we see with acute progression in sarcoidosis.'

He could find nothing in Andy's hospital records to suggest any tests on admission for Covid; he didn't know where we'd got that idea – and clearly I couldn't ask Andy. St Thomas's would try to locate in its laboratories samples taken during Andy's treatment. In the meantime, Professor Santis asked me to collate any information that might hint at a coronavirus cluster or trail around Andy and the band. So began a personal track-and-trace operation. I interrogated not only the band members and crew, but the many friends and family who had seen Andy after his return from China, whether in his music studio, over dinners, chatting with him in the ICU or keeping vigil when he could no longer speak. What could they tell me about their health in the period between Andy's return to the UK and immediately after his death?

The band reported no symptoms, but alerted me to an incident that seemed pregnant with meaning. Their tour manager – 26 and generally in robust health – had joined up with another band after China for a series of UK gigs. On 2 December, in Leeds, his companions found him in his hotel room in respiratory distress so severe that the first hospital that admitted him quickly transferred him to the better-equipped 'Jimmy's', St James's, Europe's largest teaching hospital. He remained under its care for eight days. His GP told him she believed he had coronavirus.

My sister Lise and I developed acute conjunctivitis in late January – this was later recognised as a potential marker of Covid-19. A friend who brought food and comfort during the long days and nights in ICU exhibited the fever, cough and breathlessness originally identified as the three key symptoms of the virus. Jo coughed continuously from early February. The government issued advice in March that anyone with a fever or 'new cough' should self-isolate. Hers did not qualify as new, so she continued to work and socialise. Her husband suffered from chilblains, or so-called 'Covid toe'; members of their close circle came down with fevers and coughs. There were many such stories from our friendship group.

At the start of lockdown, I had launched an online initiative #HowCanIHelp, connecting people self-isolating or shielding with volunteers to bring food and medicine. I now looked back on that time and wondered: had I been not a helper but a carrier of the virus? I ran errands myself, bringing food and medicine to some of those who got in touch, strangers and people known to me including a friend whose most likely source of infection, if Andy had coronavirus, would have been me. He comforted me after Andy died, attended Andy's memorial, then developed a high fever and cough that laid him low.

My mother gently raised the implication I tried hardest to ignore. John had died on 22 December. His underlying conditions were incurable, but he deteriorated with an unexpected speed. His cause of death is recorded as 'hospital-acquired pneumonia'. Had we brought the virus to his bedside along with our hospital grapes?

If so, there was no way we could have known, said my mother. A quick audit of the latest evidence revealed this to be a comforting fiction. The official submission by China to the World Health Organization dated the first case of the disease to 8 December, but unconfirmed reports suggested the authorities had been aware of a new virus at least twenty days before that. Clinicians who tried to raise the alarm attracted not praise but retribution from the Chinese state. After Li Wenliang, an ophthalmologist from Wuhan, sent a message warning colleagues to take precautions against the illness sweeping through the city, he received a summons to attend the Public Security Bureau, where he was asked to sign a statement: 'We solemnly warn you: If you keep being stubborn, with such impertinence, and continue this illegal activity, you will be brought to justice – is that understood?' Yes, he wrote, he understood. Li went on to contract Covid-19 and died just days after Andy.

The more I learned, the more thoughts and possibilities whirled. France's Hammar had not travelled abroad for four months before he became ill, indicating that the virus had already made landfall in Europe by December. If so, what did this mean for transmission rates? Certainly the numbers of asymptomatic carriers must be markedly higher than the current modelling assumed. How many deaths might have been prevented if China had acted more swiftly and with transparency? How many further deaths would be avoided if the public health response were guided by more and better information?

'People in this country have had enough of experts,' declared Michael Gove ahead of the 2016 Brexit referendum.

A shockingly cavalier statement from a serving cabinet minister, this reflected – and pandered to – exactly that deep mistrust of authorities and institutions that is giving a helping hand to wool-pullers across the globe. Gove's specific target was a group of economists who had warned against a self-mutilating rupture with the European Union. He wouldn't have got much traction if he'd attacked scientists instead. In researching *Amortality*, I identified two contrasting groups that gained influence as faith in other institutions and professions receded: celebrities and scientists.

When the pandemic bit, scientists themselves became celebrities, repositories not only of public trust but of that rarest of commodities: hope. 'He has fought dinosaurs, body snatchers, and aliens,' read an internet meme playing on the physical resemblance between Christian Drosten, a leading expert in coronaviruses and head of Berlin's Charité Institute of Virology, and the action movie star Jeff Goldblum. 'I'll trust him with this virus too.'

At Downing Street press conferences, Boris Johnson and his cabinet never appeared without scientists to flank them – and give them cover. Overnight Sir Patrick Vallance, the UK's Government Chief Scientific Adviser, and Chris Whitty, its Chief Medical Officer, gained household recognition and unlikely rock-star status. Professor Anthony Fauci, an eminent immunologist serving on the White House Coronavirus Task Force, emerged as a vital corrective to a president who right from the start undermined his own public health officials and plucked dangerous recommendations from the fetid air, at one official briefing proposing killing the virus in ways that would also kill the patient. Why not irradiate the body with ultra violet light or by injecting disinfectant, Trump ventured. 'As you probably noticed, the task-force meetings have not occurred as often lately,' Fauci later told a reporter. 'And certainly my meetings with the president have been dramatically decreased.'

Sweden's chief epidemiologist, Anders Tegnell, acquired a devout fanbase. 'He's just been doing his job great,' one of Tegnell's compatriots told Reuters, explaining his decision to have his hero's face tattooed on his bicep. That was before Tegnell's advice, to resist a compulsory lockdown, attracted wide censure amid Sweden's substantial Covid-19 toll, the highest in Scandinavia. Tegnell stood by his strategy; time, he said, would prove him right.

Some of these figures were always bound to topple from their pedestals. The term 'science' covers a range of disciplines and philosophies that often stand at odds with each other and rarely offer the certainty fearful populations most crave. Some branches rely on observable phenomena; others might lean on computer models. In my research for *Amortality*, I'd met quite a few men (they were all men) who built elaborate theories about extending human longevity based on nothing more intimately connected to the human experience than the life cycles of fruit flies or the grinding of algorithms.

The broad sweep of science is riven with the same inequalities and thus the same dysfunctions and skills gaps that disfigure wider society. Membership of Johnson's Scientific Advisory Group for Emergencies (SAGE) was unknown until *The Guardian* identified twenty-three participants and questioned the narrow range of scientific fields represented. The report added 'As to other measures of diversity, the gender balance of SAGE is predictably skewed, with sixteen men to seven women and only one ethnic minority person. Given that coronavirus has been shown to disproportionately affect people from Black and ethnic minority communities, the comparative lack of Black and ethnic minority experts seems a troubling omission.'

An alternative group of scientists came together to address such concerns. Called Independent SAGE and led by Sir David King, a former Chief Scientific Adviser to the government, it began to issue its own briefings. When the government published a list of more than fifty scientists contributing to official SAGE, the fuller picture was slightly more reassuring, but members themselves raised questions not just on the processes by which they formulated advice but also about its reception. Mechanisms for transmitting advice to ministers and translating it into policy appeared more convoluted than in many other countries. Angela Merkel, herself a scientist, took regular direct briefings from experts such as Christian Drosten.

The government's response was to downgrade the importance of SAGE, setting up the Joint Biosecurity Centre to coordinate the UK's Covid response. This might smooth communication lines, but the newer body has been criticised by members of both SAGE and Independent SAGE for a lack of transparency with respect to its membership, governance and accountability.

Advice, and the systems and structures for giving and receiving it, can always be improved, but decisions, in the end, rest with government. On 22 January, Professor Neil Ferguson at Imperial College's School of Public Health warned officials that Covid-19 appeared to have a high infectivity rate. To stop its spread, a lockdown would be required. Two days later, with the leading medical journal, *The Lancet*, carrying a report by Chinese doctors of an acute danger to human life from Covid-19, Boris Johnson skipped the first COBRA emergency committee meeting (the acronym is taken from the government's Cabinet

Office Briefing Rooms). He missed the second COBRA five days later and the third on 5 February, despite declarations in the intervening week by the World Health Organization of a global public health emergency and by NHS England of the first-ever level four critical incident. He swerved the fourth and fifth COBRA meetings too.

February 28 saw confirmation of the first death in the UK of a Covid patient, while a leaked government document estimated that up to 80 per cent of the population could contract the disease; half a million of these might die. A day later, the NHS sounded the alarm about severe shortages of personal protective equipment – and Johnson announced his engagement to his pregnant fiancée Carrie Symonds. The next day Johnson finally attended a COBRA meeting.

Vital time that might have been used early in the pandemic to build up supplies of PPE, ventilators and testing kits, or on building capacity in medical and testing systems and restricting the spread of the disease by stopping travel and closing down large gatherings had already been squandered. 'It should be business as usual,' said Johnson. After France cancelled sporting fixtures, the UK government said there was 'no rationale' for doing so. In mid-March 250,000 spectators attended the Cheltenham festival of racing. Seventy-six-thousand people crammed together to watch a derby between Manchester's rival football teams, City and United. Three-thousand fans of the football team Atletico Madrid flew to the UK for its match with Liverpool. Madrid had already been identified as a virus hotspot – as the Merseyside region itself then became.

Westminster insiders reported that Johnson's chief adviser Dominic Cummings appeared to be doing more hands-on leading of government than Johnson himself – though the prime minister was certainly hands-on in one respect. After SAGE warned against shaking hands, Johnson addressed a press conference. 'I'm shaking hands continuously,' he said. 'I was at a hospital the other night where I think there were actually a few coronavirus patients and I shook hands with everybody you'll be pleased to know.'

He went on to do a lot more glad-handing, at a facility working on developing a Covid antibodies test and at a Six Nations rugby match attended by 82,000 people. In late March, he tested positive for Covid. On 5 April he was admitted to St Thomas's hospital, perhaps under the treatment of the same critical care experts who had done their best for Andy. It was an odd feeling, hanging on every news bulletin, my memory wandering again through familiar corridors and wards, anxious that Johnson might die, relieved as he recovered and wondering if, perhaps, he might now understand this crisis in its human terms, lives destroyed, families torn apart.

He officially took back the reins of the UK's coronavirus response two weeks after his discharge from hospital. Cummings retained his position of influence even after revelations about his strange breaches of lockdown rules: a 264-mile journey from London to a property belonging to his father after he and his wife contracted Covid; a sixty-mile drive to 'test his eyesight'. I tried to imagine how the crisis might have played out under different – and wiser – leadership. Steering any nation through the pandemic would never have been easy. There is seldom unanimity among government advisers. Scientists will always disagree with each other. Concerns about the economic impacts of lockdown weren't wrong, even if the idea of a choice between a healthy population and a healthy economy ignored their fundamental interdependence.

In the end, though, political decisions – and the absence of political decisions – set a course that mired England ever deeper into a deadly crisis. Measured by deaths per head of population, Northern Ireland, Scotland and Wales, in exercising limited devolved powers, have so far all performed better. So have other European countries, not only well-resourced, well-prepared Germany, but threadbare Greece. According to a July 2020 report by the Office for National Statistics, England's excess death rate – the percentage increase over and above the average death rate – was the highest of the entire continent.

If and when an independent inquiry into the government's handling of the crisis convenes, a quartet of missteps are likely to attract the fiercest scrutiny. The most prominent of these is the delay in taking action. Close to six weeks elapsed between Covid being declared a serious public health risk and its classification as a notifiable disease. The government continued to drag its heels, letting those big events go ahead and deferring ordering people to stay home until 23 March while citing the danger of 'lockdown fatigue', the anticipated limited public tolerance for stay-at-home orders. A BBC investigation into this decision found that none of the scientists working in an advisory capacity claimed ownership of these warnings. Professor Ferguson later told a parliamentary committee 'Had we introduced lockdown measures a week earlier, we would have reduced the final death toll by at least a half.'

By then the UK had already stopped mass testing and contact tracing. There was a clutch of questionable decisions around that time – the lifting of restrictions on travel from known virus hotspots, including Wuhan, and the downgrading of definitions of adequate levels of PPE – but this was the most egregious. Public health authorities now worked in the dark, the true numbers of cases and levels of asymptomatic transmission unknown. 'Tracing every contact must be the backbone of the response in every country,' said the WHO. Ministers did their best to blame the failure on Public Health England. News that the government was to scrap this body and replace it with another met with scepticism. 'You don't deal with the problem of an over-centralised, dysfunctional organisation by creating another over-centralised organisation,' a former health official told the BBC. 'You don't change horses mid-stream – this pandemic has still got a long way to run.'

Ahead of that reorganisation, the government would reintroduce contact tracing, but flounder both in establishing reliable systems and guidelines for manual tracing and, most conspicuously, in delivering a digital system. Instead of building on such systems already in use in other countries, not without flaws, Britain pushed ahead in building its own app. A trial of the app on the Isle of Wight failed and other tests made clear that the app was a long way from functioning, if it ever could. 'You had a government, a machine, that was terribly eager for good news,' a Whitehall source told Sky News. 'It was a lot like 1940, the first few months. It was a bit like the Norway campaign. Go off and do something that'll be a big success – and it turns out to be a debacle.' And an expensive one.

Another decision inflicted a different and higher cost: the loss of lives, many lives. The first recorded death from Covid in a care home took place on 6 March but unrestricted visiting rights would continue until April. On 19 March, new guidance came into effect that cleared hospital beds for incoming emergencies by transferring elderly patients from hospitals to care homes without first testing them for Covid. Even after the policy was changed to include prior testing, the glaring absence of adequate testing infrastructure and sufficient PPE to shield residents and staff saw infections – and fatalities – mount. My friend assisting in a care home watched helpless as Covid took hold. One of her charges screamed in distress for three days then, as she used a hoist to lift him to change his sheets, convulsed and died. She saw a family pressed up against a ground-floor window while their mother, so close but so unreachable on the other side of the glass, took her last breath. She grieves still. So, too, my mother, learning to live without her darling John and determined to see a value to her life. She understood each care home fatality not as a number but as someone like her, judged expendable by the state. 'If I get sick,' she said to me, 'they won't do anything to save me.' I couldn't argue with her analysis.

All this pain, and here was I, contemplating a betrayal. Across the world, Andy had been celebrated as a music hero. Would he forgive me for linking his name instead with tragedy and disease? I didn't honestly know, but the imperatives of making public the questions about his death seemed to me to outweigh any personal concerns. If Covid had killed Andy, the virus had circulated earlier and wider than any of the official narratives admitted. Any current and future strategies to quell the outbreak and ease lockdown measures would be effective only if based on good data. Oh sweetheart. I'm sorry. I couldn't get past the realisation that lives and livelihoods were at stake.

The decision was tough. Once made, the choices flowing from it were obvious. I would write about my investigation into Andy's death rather than entrusting the story to another journalist; I published the piece on my blog. I chose carefully among any subsequent interview requests – and there were many. Quite a few of them seemed more interested in filming my tears than in giving a platform to urgent questions and issues. Those I declined, politely.

Just before making public my post, I contacted Professor Santis again to ensure that I had accurately represented his and his colleagues' views. He had news for me. St Thomas's had managed to find and test a lung fluid sample from Andy for Covid antigens. The test had come up negative, but this by no means ruled out a Covid infection. By the time of Andy's admission into hospital, he had been ill for weeks. The virus would likely have already left his body. Researchers were coming to understand that the pathogen typically disappears within days. Often what kills patients is the immune complications it triggers. Professor Santis suggested possible next steps: locating and screening samples from the tour manager and testing Andy's samples for antibodies. I told him that I and others who had shown Covid-like symptoms would happily submit to tests too.

Of course, even positive antibody results from anyone but Andy or his tour manager would at most be suggestive of a cluster rather than offering firm proofs. After the first rush of excitement about testing, it also became clear that the tests were less reliable than incautious reporting had suggested. *The Telegraph*, for example, hailed a new antibody test from pharmaceuticals giant Roche, stating that Public Health England had 'confirmed Roche's claim that its test is accurate in 100 per cent of cases'. The piece included a quote from an anonymous government source declaring, avidly: 'We want to get our hands on as many of these as possible.' The newspaper was by no means the only news organisation to confuse sensitivity (the percentage who test positive, from all those tested who are positive) and specificity (the percentage who test negative, from those tested who actually are negative) with accuracy – the percentage of people accurately diagnosed by the test.

Both antigen and antibody tests tend to fail in the same way – they are much more likely to return false negatives than false positives. Failures are caused if the test is administered incorrectly and for other reasons. Antigen tests are most likely to be accurate within three days of symptoms appearing; often the tests take too long to arrive and as anyone who has taken one knows, they're tricky to complete. Antibody tests on patients confirmed to have contracted Covid-19 and administered by trained staff sometimes also produce false negatives. This raises the possibility that not all patients seroconvert, that is, respond by creating antibodies.

Nick Gay helped me to understand the implications: 'A positive test is a good indicator of a past infection but a negative one is pretty meaningless,' he emailed. 'This is because in mild or moderate cases the dominant immune response is what we term T-helper 1, mediated by CD8+ T cells that recognise and kill infected cells, but they do not produce circulating antibodies and likely not long-lived memory cells that will protect against second infections.' He added a further clarification in case I had missed the import of his words. 'This is why the development of a vaccine is very uncertain and is not the panacea some media make it out to be.'

Not all press reporting fell into this trap. Many journalists did an excellent job of conveying the complexities of the science as well as the politics. *The Guardian* commissioned Frances Perraudin, who had worked with me at *TIME* magazine, to try to track down cases that could demonstrate beyond doubt that Covid arrived in the UK ahead of the official dates. I did my best to help her, using social media to invite anyone to get in touch who had tested positive for antibodies after suffering a Covid-like illness before the pandemic was declared. People were anyway already sharing their stories. My blog about Andy had been read close to 34,000 times and an interview I gave to the BBC's Coronavirus Newscast, ran as a standalone programme, generating a huge response.

Quite a few of my correspondents offered nothing more substantial than tales of flu-like illness the previous winter. A smaller number provided more compelling testimony. A woman called Debra Scott succumbed after her husband's school reunion in November to a virus that bore some of the now-familiar Covid traits – the wracking cough and apparent recovery followed by a sudden deterioration. She subsequently tested positive for antibodies. Research scientists and medical professionals sought me out too. 'We all knew something was going on,' a GP told me. 'We had meetings in the practice about it back in December.'

I published a new blog post, detailing one of the most convincing accounts. The protagonists did not wish to be identified, but hoped to assist with research into Covid timelines, so I gave them pseudonyms, Patrick and Daniel.

If, as they believe, they are Covid survivors, they contracted the virus in the UK. They had last travelled abroad more than three months before they became ill. On New Year's Eve, Patrick confided to Daniel that he felt too rough to go out to dinner. 2020 brought fever and the loss of two senses, taste and smell. Daniel also got sick, but his symptoms were milder and his recovery swift. Patrick continued to decline.

A few miles away, I watched Andy with deepening concern. By 18 January, Daniel and I would both conclude that our husbands needed urgent medical attention, though the only symptom shared by Patrick and Andy was a high temperature.

Patrick complained that January weekend of a fresh symptom, peripheral neuropathy, pins-and-needles. Then one side of his face froze. Doctors retreated from an initial diagnosis of Bell's palsy after the paralysis spread to the other side of his face, accompanied by an acute inflammation to the back of the head. A second diagnosis followed: Guillain-Barré syndrome, a rare and serious condition that sometimes proves fatal and has now been identified as an occasional complication of Covid-19. Patrick, admitted to hospital, would not go home until the end of January. As he prepared for release from hospital, St Thomas's staff conferred with me about releasing my beloved from life support.

Patrick's evidence for the earlier arrival of Covid in the UK remains for now, and like the other stories I collected, circumstantial and anecdotal, though he has tested positive for antibodies. His test, conducted in May at a London teaching hospital, reacted slowly. The administering clinician told him this suggested that the antibodies had been in Patrick's system for a considerable while, months rather than weeks. At time of writing, samples taken from him during his hospital stay have not been tested for antigens. The UK's earliest confirmed case of community transmission is currently a Nottingham woman, who tested positive on 21 February, and died on 3 March, the day before Andy's memorial. A coroner's report on a man called Peter Attwood, issued more than seven months after the 84-year-old's death on 30 January, listed Covid-19 as his cause of death. Reportedly the virus had been detected in his tissue samples. A positive result for Patrick's tissues would irrefutably challenge the UK's pandemic timelines.

Some months ago I wondered if further investigation into Andy's case might do this. Now I am learning to live with the certainty of uncertainty. In August, my blood was tested for antibodies. The GP described my negative result with a phrase that has become increasingly familiar: the result was, she said, 'meaningless', given how much time had elapsed and how mild my case would have been. Later the same month, Andy's specialist confirmed that St Thomas's could make no further headway with their investigation into his death. 'The virology department have not been able to identify material they can test for antibodies,' Professor Santis emailed. 'Sadly, the final piece of the puzzle remains elusive.'

Would I feel better if he had written, instead, with a firm post-mortem diagnosis? I can't say. What matters, what lacerates, is that Andy and John are gone. I only ever wanted to find out what killed them in order to improve understanding of the virus. This understanding is still deficient, but the gaps are being filled by researchers with resources and skills far beyond mine. Many of the evolving theories reset the timelines in China and beyond; others unpick the workings of the disease.

A report published in August in the scientific journal *Cell* found that 29 per cent of samples from blood donated before the pandemic had cross-reactive T cells to the Covid-19 spike protein – which could either point to infection by different coronaviruses or suggest that SARS-CoV-2 was in circulation well before its official debut in Wuhan. The same report found that although people infected with Covid and showing mild or no symptoms might not develop antibodies, they were likely to produce T cells that granted some protection against severe reinfection. This might mean that testing for antibodies underestimates both the spread of Covid and of resistance to it. The importance of T cells in fighting infection indicated 'a previously unanticipated degree of population-level immunity against Covid-19', the authors wrote. Some will interpret these findings to mean that the Swedish man with Anders Tegnell's face on his bicep can wear a short-sleeved shirt with pride. Yet in many parts of the world infections, and deaths, are soaring and there is increasing evidence for 'long Covid', a series of symptoms such as chronic fatigue and loss of smell that affect some Covid patients for many months after they are supposedly free from the virus. In a separate development, recovered patients are contracting Covid again, casting doubt on the idea that infection confers immunity. One, in Hong Kong, discovered this mischance through an airport screening. He was feeling fine. Another, in the US, developed symptoms that were more severe the second time round.

Capricious Covid continues to keep researchers guessing but this much is clear. No longer is it disputed that many Covid cases, perhaps a majority, like the Hong Kong patient's second bout, are asymptomatic. The disease could never have been contained simply by isolating those with coughs and fevers. Antigen testing and contact tracing will remain vital to an effective public health response unless and until an effective vaccine is widely deployed or treatments developed that significantly reduce the impact of the disease on those made vulnerable by age or underlying conditions. An effective programme is needed now, not at some point in the gleaming future invoked by Boris Johnson under the label 'Operation Moonshot'. His hypothetical, hyperbolic scheme to test millions daily, as journalist Jessica Elgot pointed out on Twitter, would cost £100 billion, a figure that is 'absolutely wild. It's double the entire defence budget, it's two-thirds of what the government spends a year on the entire NHS'. The British Medical Association swiftly highlighted another reason for scepticism. Laboratories in the UK were already struggling to process the relatively small numbers of tests currently being carried out. In September, with children returning to school and infection rates rising, the testing system sagged and gave way, with no testing capacity available at all outside hospitals and care settings. In October, Boris Johnson admitted that 15,481 confirmed Covid cases had not been logged in daily totals or passed on for contact tracing during the previous ten critical days as a second wave of Covid surged amid discussions of the need for further lockdowns. He blamed a computer glitch. Later that same month, as cases and hospitalisations spiked again, especially in the North of England, he introduced a confusing new tier system of restrictions. Minutes released by SAGE on the same day revealed he had resisted the advice of his scientific advisers three weeks earlier to implement immediate measures to stop the spread of Covid.

Still I push for answers, but my questions are different. I joined Covid-19 Bereaved Families for Justice UK and campaign with them for an independent judge-led inquiry with a rapid review phase into the government handling of the pandemic to draw learnings from its mistakes and illuminate the systemic and structural failings in urgent need of addressing. The group also calls for better mental health care provision for those in grief and trauma, a gaping void discussed in the next chapter. One member, Dr Cathy Gardner, whose father died in a care home, is crowdfunding legal proceedings against the government on the basis that its policies with regard to Covid and care homes breached its legal duty to protect citizens.

There are longer-term concerns to address too. Horrible phrases infect public debate: war metaphors mingle uneasily with talk of a 'covexit' and a 'new normal'. If I have learned anything from observing the world as a journalist and trying to change it as an activist, it's that this so-called new normal will benefit the majority only if we do everything within our power to design it for the majority. The burning question for me, therefore, is how best we should do this. With populism in the ascendancy and trust on the slide, I'm honestly not sure. News just a month ahead of the US presidential election that Donald Trump himself had contracted Covid sparked an epidemic of scepticism and a rash of conspiracy theories. It's hard enough to construct the foundations of a better future; all the more so when nothing appears solid.

Here's what I can tell you: time without Andy will never feel as meaningful as time with him; my mother is adrift without John – but time has the value we give it. In looking for answers as a journalist, working for that better future through activism, and seeing through to completion Andy's final, brilliant projects, I am resolved to make my time count for something. So too my mother. With this book, we hope in our own small way to help others.

The fifth letter to John

1 July 2020

Dear John,

For the first time in years and years, I have found myself contemplating the earlier tragedies and loss in my life. Recently I overheard a *Desert Island Discs* guest say that the death of his mother sent him into such profound shock that he was unable to inhabit a normal social life until he was at university. As she had died when he wasn't there (in a road accident), he often refused to leave the house lest another such traumatic loss occur. He was 12.

As you know all too well, it was at the same age that I saw my father die of a coronary in his bedroom on a sunny Sunday morning in July. With my 10-year-old brother, Kenny, standing next to me, we heard him say to my mother, 'Ruth, I don't feel very well.' He put his hand to his chest and toppled over backwards in one piece. It was obvious he was dead, even as he hit the floor. My mother very calmly and capably got us dressed and took us next door; when she came back for us in the late afternoon and informed us that our father was dead, we already knew. He was just 41 years old.

Two years later, almost to the day, I was called home from a week staying with my best friend to be greeted by a weeping mother and told that Kenny was dead. At a summer camp in the Rocky Mountains, he had been struck by lightning at an end-of-term barbecue. Electrical storms come up very suddenly in the high mountains and this one arrived when the boys were in an exposed meadow. They were running for shelter when the bolt hit my brother and badly burned the boy running next to him.

I am sure this double tragedy caused me huge grief, but I forced it underground as I was just starting high school and wanted to fit in. Even then, I could not stand people expressing sympathy for me and my doubly deprived mother. I wanted none of it. I do not remember weeping for either father or brother or, after a short time, missing them very much.

I later lost my two best university friends before they were 30, one to suicide and the other to a rare form of encephalitis. Both left small children behind. I worried that all these deaths would make me clingy and frightened as a mother, but they did not. I was and always have been motivated by a desire to be 'normal', which for me means outgoing, cheerful, actively social and involved with my work and friends. By the time our recent tragedies occurred: Sarah in 2016, Maurice the following year, then you and Andy, I was much older and more vulnerable but still fought for the same kind of normality. I have largely remained dry-eyed, outgoing, connected and fairly calm. That has partly been possible because, as I did all those years ago, I fight to keep a lot of the turmoil inside and relegate it to my dreams (which are turbulent).

It does break through in the daytime too, though, no matter how hard I try. I am finding that grief is tricky and complicated. It is not like a pain or an ache and no form of paracetamol will wish it away. It lies in ambush and all sorts of things will trigger bursts of anguish for which no medication can be prescribed. I banished my memories of my father and brother for so long, but I cannot deny your absence. Though I haven't yet seen your ghost, your presence is so real that I talk to you every day and think about you every minute.

But like Ruth, the mother you taught me to appreciate after years of pushing her away, I knew from day one without you that I had to roll up my sleeves and get to work – learning the things I had left you to manage, running the house sensibly, getting through probate and sorting out my US affairs and not shouting for help whenever things go wrong, although I still have tendencies in that direction as my daughters will attest. Ruth, unlike me, seemed – at least to my younger self – theatrical in her grief, particularly when Kenny died, but she wasn't that way for long. She knew where the buck stopped, and so do I.

I have also begun to accept that I was unduly critical of her. Ruth had lost her own father when she was barely 2, so entirely grew up without one. Her parents had driven her and her five siblings from Kansas to Colorado in a horse-drawn carriage, in the hopes that the mountain air would cure her father's tuberculosis. Instead her mother Ida Mary was left in a strange place, without friends and family, coping with widowhood and her consider- able brood. This was Ruth's background. When my father, Lewis, died so suddenly, she needed to be practical and take over management of the household and children without delay, and that is what she did.

In the many losses I have suffered, I have not yet lost a child. You went through that terrible loss very recently and I do not know how you managed your grief over Sarah. We did not talk about it very much. I am sure Ruth's grief over Kenny was overwhelming. Her beautiful and bright son, whom she had sent to that camp in the mountains, was dead.

Her grieving went on for years. She slept with several men, some of them old family friends, as she was desperate to get pregnant, but the tragedy may have tipped her into menopause. She considered adopting a lad via a settlement house in Chicago, a charity offering food and shelter, and invited two or three to live with us in the quiet suburbs to see if the arrangement could work longer term, but they proved uncontrollable, and often ran away. They were no replacement for her son.

I will admit, I was jealous. My mother had unwisely told me when I was far too young that my father had wanted a son, was disappointed that his firstborn was a daughter and wouldn't rest until that baby boy duly appeared. I felt her behaviour might be a continuation of that prejudice. If I had died instead of Kenny, would her despair have been as profound?

When Ruth eventually found happiness again with her second husband, Leo, I initially gave her a hard time for marrying someone I did not know. They had met while I was away at university. Nevertheless I grew to love Leo. He contracted Parkinson's much later in the marriage, while I was living in England and not able to help. One day, Ruth found him tucked up in bed next to an empty bottle of pills and, on his desk, a sane and comprehensive note about his affairs. I mourned Leo from the other side of the ocean, but already had a family and my own life to lead.

While twin widowhood has brought me closer to my youngest daughter, Ruth's and my losses seemed to drive us apart. I gave her no help, no support, very little kindness until I met you. You did not get to know Ruth until she was old, ill and had few years to live but I marvel at how quickly you understood her and how good you were to her.

So now while I grieve for you, I am also grieving not so much for Ruth, who has been dead for nearly forty years, but for the relationship we never built. She loved me very much, but we were never close. Only now do I regret that.

Middle age has been described as the moment you look in a mirror and see your parent of the same sex. There is so much of Ruth in me, and I have struggled so hard to deny it. But it is her pioneer strength and genes which are powering me now as I fight my way through bereavement under lockdown.

As I say, this has been at the forefront of my mind, and even more so this morning as I write, because of two significant milestones. Today is the one hundredth day since lockdown restrictions were imposed. Plus, we have finally been promised some further easing of restrictions from this Saturday, 4 July. As an American that date has always been meaningful, the Independence Day that from childhood I celebrated with my family as the date we rid ourselves of you British. This 4th of July I will instead mourn my independence from you, while trying to comfort myself at the prospect of the lifting of some restrictions. The new rules will not extend to Leicester, which is experiencing a flare-up of new Covid cases and is back under full lockdown. I expect a similar return to strict rules in London as for weeks very few people seem to have been obeying any of the distancing regulations and recently there have been all sorts of raves and parties with young people mingling closely.

The independence for me is anyway limited, as many people including our family are trying to stay safe by minimising our contacts with the outside world. One weird thing which just happened is that I received a letter from HM Government to say that as a vulnerable, shielded person who had been entirely housebound for the 100 days, I could now go outdoors but would sacrifice the state benefits which had accrued to my shielded status. I never got the original letter nor accepted that I was shielded, despite what our daughters said, so have regularly gone outside – for walks, shopping, collecting the newspaper and, more recently, garden meetings with friends, family and neighbours. Nor had I enjoyed the listed benefits, so no loss to me, but how indicative of the sloppy government handling of the pandemic. I wonder when I will trust the situation enough to take public transport or go out socially. I need to see the dentist and have my hair cut but am not doing so now because I would have to travel into central London. I have not yet even been as far as our bank.

The big achievement of this week is that Isaac sold your motorised scooter on eBay to an elderly couple outside London. Their son, a lorry driver, collected it (not in his lorry but a very bright orange VW) to drive it up to them. I had spotted one set of tiny keys in your desk drawer but not the all-important ignition key which is in the post to them now.

Joanie came over on Sunday to talk to Catherine and me about end of life planning. It was her intervention in what remained of your life (last summer, about six months before you died) that saved our lives if not yours. She had successfully got you to fill in a form with your end of life wishes as well as important information about your investments and direct debits which showed us the way forward in those dark January days when you suddenly weren't here to tell us.

I have really learnt that a practical understanding of what to expect in bereavement appears to be much lacking. Only about one third of adult Brits have a Will or any notion of leaving their affairs in good order for those who have to clear up after a loved or even an unloved one dies. I am spending almost as much time clearing up my own end of life planning in both the UK and USA as I am in executing your probate and digging out all that financial information I declined to keep abreast of when you were alive and here to answer questions. As a highly independent career woman – there it is again, that idea of independence – how could I have let this happen? Yet people of every sort do, as the statistics attest.

Joanie is fascinating. She also runs a regular so-called Death Café. I will certainly attend when they begin again. The meetings are free and open to anyone who wants to talk about death and dying. At each table is a trained interlocutor to keep conversation flowing. For the past few months, the elephant in every room has been coronavirus. But the constant primal fear and elephant in all rooms is death. You and I didn't talk about it or prepare for it as much as we should have done. I locked away all those thoughts about Ruth and about my father and Kenny. Andy did not have a Will because he could not contemplate talking about or planning for his death. This is a major reason people do not have Wills and Power of Attorney arrangements. Even though some of us will escape the virus, death is unavoidable and often does not even respect chronological order. I am now evangelistic about begging people to overcome their fears and scruples, talk to their nearest and dearest and organise for life beyond their own lives. This is what Death Cafés are for – to talk freely and to help people of all ages to embrace the certainty of death and make provision for it.

I know you often thought your life had not lived up to your own high expectations and ambition. You wanted to be an opera singer but were discouraged by your father and your need to make a living. When you got into financial services, you wanted to be the boss so you could change the way companies were run, especially their sales forces. But you ended up running the sales forces and often being obstructed by the boss. You were desperate to be an MP and never got there, although you served on two county councils and two hospital boards, one as lead governor. You wanted to paint like a modern Cézanne; you were a good painter but not quite in his league!

You were, however, in a league of your own, my darling. If only you knew how many people you touched and helped and who ask after my welfare knowing I have lost a jewel without price. You were kind and loving and wanted the world to be better for all. You loved beauty in all forms and left it behind in your garden and your art. You always cared, which is a rare quality. With so much to dislike in today's world, how wonderful to have such loving memories as the constant companion in my eternal loneliness.

Love,
Anne

Chapter 8: Comfort

Too soon? This was Sandi Toksvig's catchphrase after Andy died. My Women's Equality Party co-founder had visited him in the ICU, pretended to test new stand-up material on him as he lay in a coma and made absolutely sure I knew she'd always be on hand with limitless friendship and inappropriate jokes. The first of these, post-mortem, related to the heterosexuality she regarded (however much she loved Andy) as my misfortune. With Andy gone, I could finally change sides, she deadpanned, then waited a beat. 'Too soon, darling?'

Humour us, we who are grieving. It is never too soon for comedy, never too soon to give us glimpses of light. Don't tiptoe around us for fear of doing or saying the wrong thing. Authentic conversation is what we crave. Sorrow strips away artifice. Loss makes us yearn for real connection – and a laugh. We need to laugh.

While there are spectacularly tin-eared comments a person might make – and my mother and I have compiled a few, choice examples for the last chapter of this book – it is always better to speak as you feel, always better to say and do something rather than nothing. The bloopers in their own way provided hours of pleasure. I still chuckle at the memory of friends trying to dig themselves out of verbal holes, their inadvertent exhortations to us widows to 'get well soon!' as if grief were a lurgy to be shaken off with paracetamol and bed rest; the well-meaning acquaintance of many years who mused aloud about whether Andy's death would make me regret my choice to remain childless, then, in horrified realisation at what she'd just said, offered to loan me her kids. Another friend signed off his condolence letter with a phrase that made me howl, with grief and laughter: 'Tell Andy to say hi to John and Sara B.'

Better this, by far, than silence. However scary you find our grief, please don't ghost those of us learning to live with ghosts. Invite us for lunches, drinks and dinners, offer to include us in your clunky Zoom quizzes. We can always say no. Let us listen to the assembled company rather than demanding to know how we're doing. Those of you as yet unblemished by loss cannot begin to grasp how much comfort there is to be squeezed from the moments that allow us to feel almost normal.

Most friends and family instinctively did and said lovely, helpful things; I would guess the majority of people do. In the few weeks before lockdown banished them, well-wishers sought out my mother and me, coaxed us to take walks or relax with them. They didn't shy from the terrible space next to us, inside us, accepting its presence without embarrassment. Perhaps they already saw what we could not, a shimmering. Over time, the space fills with particles of love and memory, resolving into a constant, welcome companion. John and Andy are gone but they sit beside us.

Then again, we are exceptionally lucky, my mother and I. We are cushioned by decades of happiness, seven between us, and we have each other. Incomprehensible though it is to find ourselves bereft, losers at a time of global loss, how much more difficult to go through this alone? Our weekly meetings enable us to name our feelings and experiences, to share small triumphs and setbacks. They are a form of talking therapy and, for now, that seems enough.

This may not always be the case. Grief and its ugly sibling, trauma, could yet undo us. We observe ourselves making progress according to self-determined metrics: we cry less, smile more, feel a little more confident in our own abilities and some kind of future. Tomorrow might knock us for six. The mother who waited for me, distraught, the day she was targeted by fraudsters wasn't the mother of my previous visit, flexing independent wings, not yet ready to fly but close.

Lise and I were able to offer her immediate practical assistance and some reassurance. It was fortunate that we were in a position to do so, self-employed and living, by London standards, nearby. Even so, it's not always possible to drop everything. We too are dealing with a lot right now, busy and grieving. Our mother's needs might have clashed with ours. Moreover we could have done or said something that made her feel worse. Neither my sister nor I possess any formal training in bereavement, just rather too much experience of it, plus a bit of knowledge gleaned from our recent counselling sessions.

It had been my idea, soon after Andy died, to ask Lise and Cassie to join me for counselling with an integrative psychotherapist called Pauline Rennie-Peyton. I had seen Pauline once or twice after the deaths, within a month, of Sarah and Sara B. Years before that, Andy and I had consulted her together to repair the damage wrought by the loss of Michael and Paula. That period of my life, more than any other, had schooled me in the dangers of assuming I could always heal myself.

Cassie appeared to be coping with Maurice's death, but she is private and stoic and it's easy to expect too much from her.

Looking through old WhatsApps, I discovered I had updated her in real time on the morning I called the ambulance for Andy. The messages must have been distressing for her in the extreme; she is someone who meets challenges by doing things and there was nothing, in those hours, to be done. Later she was able to sit with Andy, keep him company on his first Sunday morning in hospital, reading the papers with him and diverting him from his discomfort with a debate about exactly how much is the right amount of chocolate on a cappuccino. She spent a more difficult Sunday with him too, when he could barely speak. Even then she thought he'd pull through. After the doctors told us he would not, she turned to me with a desolate question. 'How did we get here?'

When the pain is too sharp, Cassie becomes, in her own words, 'stony'; she closes down. With Maurice she made a huge difference not only to his life but his death, nursing him at home, attending him every day in hospice. Towards the end, she concealed her grief, giving so little away that he would ask friends how she was, what she was feeling. Recently another bereavement turned her to stone. When her beautiful grey mare Peaches was diagnosed with a condition that would render movement increasingly uncomfortable, Cassie made the torturous decision to have her euthanised. We spent Peaches's last full day giving her the best time we could, a hay net studded with apples and carrots, a stroll under fading skies.

Lise, too, had endured a series of significant losses and challenges and now this, two men she and Cassie adored, gone within a month of each other. I watched my sisters trying to support our mother and me at their own expense. Automatically they assumed their grief to be less urgent than ours, less important according to some unspoken hierarchy. Perhaps, I suggested, we might find mutual consolation in talking together about these things.

By now lockdown had confined us to our homes, so we met with Pauline via Zoom, Tuesday evenings, for one hour. The sessions proved eye-opening. It wasn't so much that Pauline said anything profound; it was that her expert stewardship of the conversation led each of us to new understandings.

After the hour was up, Pauline would leave while we lingered online, continuing our dialogue or just chatting. After a few weeks, we began to convene without Pauline, inviting Catherine A to join us. Even now, we four meet most weeks. Grief, isolating in isolation, has brought us ever closer together.

A fresh acquaintance, Kathryn de Prudhoe, is explaining the deficiencies of the UK's mental health provision to me. This isn't an area I've ever researched, but the story is horribly familiar, reflecting every area of social care, vital services sustained by determination and the unpaid labour of those, a majority women, who can least afford to work for free. The NHS already struggled to meet demand for mental health support before the pandemic dramatically inflated the numbers, including NHS staff themselves, seeking help from its services. So much grief there is these days, for the dead and for things lost – jobs, businesses, conviviality, the illusion of certainty. Charities cannot hope to fill the gaps in provision, reliant on volunteers, many still in training. Queues for free counselling stretch to the horizon. Cruse, a charity offering free bereavement counselling, told Kathryn she'd have to wait six weeks for a first appointment. The only sure way to bypass the queues is to pay for private consultations, as my sisters and I did. Kathryn decided to go this route too. This option, as she points out, is closed to many of the people who most urgently need help, especially in a world scarred by Covid. Poverty and discrimination are additional risk factors not only for the virus but for mental health impacts. 'If you're not coming from a place of being grounded and solid in the world, the risk may be higher, and you don't have emotional resources to process that,' she says. 'People already suffering racism and other forms of oppression and abuse are also more likely to be more traumatised.'

We're discussing Kathryn's involvement in the pressure group Covid-19 Bereaved Families for Justice UK. I joined the group with trepidation; I don't know whether Covid killed Andy. I quickly realised that many members may never get full or satisfactory answers either. In the first months of pandemic, only a fraction of the thousands of people dying outside hospitals were tested for Covid.

Like Pauline, Kathryn is an integrative psychotherapist. She specialises in interpersonal trauma – this could relate to any relationship at any age or stage, she says, but childhood trauma is particularly potent, shaping our world view and behaviours. As she speaks, I think of my mother and that double, gut-punching loss of her father and brother. Recently my mother wondered aloud if she might be autistic, a question prompted by her implacable resistance to any change to her routines. Surely this instinct could just as easily be a phenomenon of her traumatic early history. Kathryn concurs. 'The effect of something like that on the brain and on physiology is profound.'

Her concerns about the long-term effects of trauma, left untreated, impelled Kathryn to take an active role in the Covid-19 Bereaved Families campaign. She is spearheading the group's demands from government of proper funding for specialist mental health care for people scarred by the pandemic.

Bereavement counselling isn't just hard to come by; for many of the Covid bereaved, it won't be the appropriate form of care. 'Bereavement and grief are one thing,' she says. 'Loss is a normal and natural part of life. Our brains are set to cope, though it's not easy.'

Trauma behaves differently. Traumatic events refuse to slip into long-term memory in the way of normal recollections, instead altering the way we perceive the world and priming our brains to be on constant alert for dangers. 'Anything that recalls the trauma, that looks suspicious, sends us into a fight/ flight response. If you've been in a hospital with all the smells and sights and sounds, you might become phobic about going into a hospital,' Kathryn explains. 'When we've experienced trauma our cognitive processes can disconnect from our physical ones because it's so painful. We may not recognise our reactions for what they are.' Talking therapies tend to be effective for grief – people need to tell their stories – but only for some forms and manifestations of trauma. Other patients may need different approaches such as EMDR, eye movement desensitisation and reprocessing, designed to facilitate the processing of traumatic memories.

On the private Facebook page for the Covid-19 Bereaved Families, members of the group trade heartrending stories, raw and recent losses compounded by the rules to combat the virus and by institutional failings they hold in part responsible for the deaths. They watched, helplessly and at enforced distance, as Covid engulfed care homes. They called ambulances only to see relatives spirited away. They could not be with people they loved as they died, nor could they celebrate them in death. Fear of contagion meant sealed coffins, prohibitions on favourite clothes and mementoes and toys for the dead, no embalming to enable the final viewings that might, at least, have persuaded those in stunned denial to accept that the person they loved had really died.

This troubles Kathryn, the idea that Tony isn't really dead at all. Tony was her stepfather but so close were they that she calls him 'Dad' and clarifies their relationship only because he was just fifteen years older than she, 60 at the time of his death. A retired civil engineer, he and Kathryn's mother Joyce divided their time between homes in Leeds and rural France. On 13 March, he flew back to England. There had been no cases of Covid recorded in their French village; there still haven't. Somewhere between the start of his journey and lockdown, he caught the virus. The whole family succumbed, Kathryn too.

After two weeks laid low with flu-like symptoms, everyone but Tony showed signs of improvement. Joyce called 111, as per government guidance, then their GP, to discuss her concerns about his failure to bounce back. Both times the advice was that his symptoms were moderate. He should stay home. On 11 April, he became disoriented, took a bad fall. 'Once he'd gone in the ambulance, Mum never saw him again,' says Kathryn. Lockdown had already separated her from her dad and would prevent her from hugging her mother in their shared grief.

Admitted to Leeds General Infirmary, Tony tested positive for Covid. Doctors also detected a bleed on the brain and evidence of a heart attack. He died three days later. Kathryn was with her mother when the call came through, sitting at a two-metre distance in the garden. After the news, the women maintained their distance, and this wasn't the only disconnection. War dead, their bodies so often unrecovered, get a cenotaph – the word means 'empty tomb' – to celebrate them and as a focal point for grieving. As yet, there is no equivalent for the Covid bereaved. 'For at least the next six weeks, I kept expecting him to come home. I knew cognitively that he was gone but…' Kathryn's voice trails into silence.

She gave a statement to a local paper. 'I never imagined for one minute that this would happen. My dad was strong and fit and healthy and he lived every day to its fullest. It was really hard not being able to say goodbye, but we are going to remember him as he always was instead of how he was at the end. The really difficult part is the funeral, because he was a man who loved a party and a drink and he loved people. Hundreds of people would want to come and they can't, and that is a really poor send-off for someone who was loved by so many. The days ahead without him are going to be hard but I know that I'll be OK. My dad gave me everything I need to get through this – I'm standing on the shoulders of a giant.'

You might misread her words as acceptance, but Kathryn had begun to question the policy decisions that left Tony vulnerable, including a failure to identify his high blood pressure as a risk factor. She believes the list of people shielding from Covid should have been more comprehensive. She also points to the Nightingale hospitals, built in a blaze of publicity as the answer to a potential shortage of ICU space, then left empty. 'In China they put people with mild and moderate symptoms in hospitals.' When she saw an article in *The Guardian* about the newly formed organisation, Covid-19 Bereaved Families for Justice UK, she signed up straight away. She takes some comfort in membership of the group itself – a community nobody wished to join; the chance to talk to others who understand, who really understand – and there is, undeniably, a therapeutic benefit to activism. None of us can change what has been, but we celebrate our loved ones in seeking to protect others.

*

What to do with Andy's shoes? There are so many pairs, gorgeously aged leather, pointed boots, trainers fraying in exactly the same spot where his big toe seems to have pushed upwards like a seedling towards light. There are terry-cloth slippers, some in their original cellophane and bearing the monograms of hotel chains. He not only harvested every mini-shampoo and soap from the places he stayed; my hunter-gatherer would return triumphant from longer tours with five, ten pairs of slippers. Our bed cantilevers from a platform over storage cupboards, but his shoes never made it into those cupboards, instead piling up against them. I should move them, but where?

When this question obsessed me in the weeks after his death, I didn't yet know this was a common preoccupation for the bereaved. Despite the profusion of lovely dead in my life, I hadn't ever tried to analyse the bereavement experience or read the literature. I couldn't shake the feeling that there were all sorts of things a widow should be getting on with. Time, surely, to dump the shoes as a declaration of faith in an Andyless future. Time to start managing and channelling grief. Time to get stronger. I remembered the journalist Poorna Bell, who in the aftermath of her husband's suicide realised how much she had depended on him in their domestic life to move and carry heavy items. She had taken up powerlifting, pursuing the sport to competitive level.

Exercise had long been a part of my life, pushing away any depression and anxiety, offsetting the damage of days and nights at the computer. For decades, well before it became fashionable, I had taken weekly Pilates lessons and also practised most days on my own. When lockdown closed fitness studios, I started classes via Zoom. These turned out to be surprisingly effective, but were not without incident or difficulty. Quite a few exercises open up the chest. I'd remember too late that the tightness across my collarbones warned of unshed tears. It didn't help that I was looking up at Andy. The largest open floor space in our flat is right below the shelf I chose for his ashes, still in their earthenware wine flagon and far too heavy for me to move, even if I wanted to do so.

I could never be a powerlifter – my joints are hypermobile, bendy in ways that made for party tricks when I was younger (I used to cross my feet behind my head) but always this suppleness came at the expense of strength. Now age was beginning to repay my show-offery with aches and pains, while grief did its work too, melting solid flesh, whether muscle or scant padding, into dew. I was scrawny and weakened, but at least I could walk. The rules of lockdown dictated a single period of exercise a day. As I pushed the limits of this permission, travelling further, ignoring the pain in my feet, sacrificing toenails, I told myself this was therapy. One morning I woke to my right foot throbbing and twice its usual size. A remote consultation with my GP concluded with a prescription for penicillin and an injunction not to overdo things. Putting one foot in front of another certainly gets you a long way – but not necessarily in the right direction.

Friends kept recommending exercise of a different kind, for the soul. I'd done the counselling with my sisters and began tentatively to explore other kinds of self-help. Options such as Death Cafés, the discussion groups facilitated by my mother's friend Joanie, appealed, but these were off the menu during lockdown except as online events. I craved something that didn't flicker and buffer.

Books about grief seemed an obvious alternative. Some are written by clinicians, others, like this memoir I had yet to imagine writing, from experience. A widow of two years' standing urged me to read Megan Devine's *It's OK That You're Not OK*, which ticks both of these boxes; Devine, a psychotherapist, lost her partner to drowning. External expectations could be oppressive, my friend explained; people tended to imagine grief as a process with a beginning, middle and end and would probably pivot around the six-month mark from encouraging me to let it all hang out to intimating it was high time that I moved on. Devine's book had helped my friend to accept that she still hurt, still mourned, might never stop and bore no obligation to do so. I bought the book and another called *The Other Side of Sadness*, by George A. Bonanno, described by the *New York Times* in these encouraging terms: 'Don't worry, he says. When the worst possible news breaks, you will almost certainly get through it unscathed. Almost everyone does.' Unscathed? Really?

On the same shopping spree, I also acquired two memoirs I'd always meant to read: C. S. Lewis's *A Grief Observed* and Joan Didion's *The Year of Magical Thinking*, plus *Chase the Rainbow*, Poorna Bell's investigation into her husband's life and death. The thumbnails of the book covers appeared in my Kindle, but I didn't download the texts. Now didn't seem the right time, especially for the memoirs. Frankly I had enough grief of my own to work through without stopping to wallow in someone else's.

Anyway, I couldn't focus. If you're reading this book in the first flush of bereavement, I salute you and wonder at your resilience. Books can be great sources of comfort and guidance – voices that reassure you that you are not crazed or that, in fact, you are, with sorrow – but they require a level of attention that early-stage grief impedes. Just as it took me some time to be able to write again, so I had to find my way back to reading. I started with audiobooks. Val McDermid and Ian Rankin were the first to break the empty silence of our flat. That their stories conformed to a certain formula added to the appeal – the good always survived, however battered; mysteries around deaths would be resolved.

Later as I returned to a wider range of genres and connected once more with the printed word, still I skirted Devine and Bonanno, Lewis and Didion. I was especially wary of the latter pair. By now I had committed to writing *Good Grief* with my mother and always, as an author, I have avoided while producing a first draft any books that might knock me off course. Authors are jackdaws, drawn to shiny phrases and nuggets of insight. I didn't want to find I had embedded in the text elements filched like soaps from a hotel bathroom and I also feared comparisons. There is little more dispiriting for writers than toiling at their screens only to stumble across something of such compass and superiority that anything else on the subject seems superfluous. It wasn't until I was well beyond halfway through writing my parts of this book that I dared to examine my purchases of several months earlier.

Of course Lewis and Didion are brilliant. Of course they say things I've tried with lesser skills to articulate or have yet to form into communicable observations. There are key differences too, to each other as well as to me. Lewis expects to find solace in religious faith, grapples with God when He fails to come through. Didion, raised Episcopalian, described her views thus: 'I don't disbelieve; I just don't believe. It is an agnostic position.' To me, brought up as an atheist, the idea of resurrection has never seemed anything other than a palliative fiction.

Yet what leapt out from the pages, again and again, were

commonalities of grief, experiences and ways of thinking that loss alone engenders. Lewis is to be found musing on the rituals of sorrow, 'visiting graves, keeping anniversaries, leaving the empty bedroom exactly as "the departed" used to keep it, mentioning the dead either not at all or always in a special voice, or even (like Queen Victoria) having the dead man's clothes put out for dinner every evening'. He resists these rituals as barriers to remembering the unvarnished person. Just as I push back against others' projections of Andy and my brain's own tendency to omit and elide, so Lewis fights to preserve the wonderful unpredictability that characterised his relationship with his dead wife and defines all living love. Death has already won the first round. It wins again if we allow it to turn our independently minded beloveds into Stepford spouses, moving docile and robotic along the aisles of our faulty memories.

Didion broaches another issue that routinely confronts the grieving: what to do with all the stuff. From one day to the next, banal household items acquire a new meaning. Andy's comb has become a reliquary, the hair in its teeth the most sacred of artifacts. Quite a few religious traditions anticipate this problem, setting out timelines for grieving and rituals for the observance of grief. A friend from the Philippines tells me that its Christian communities mourn for a year, clearing belongings only at the end of that period. Secular friends urge me, within days or weeks, to get shot of Andy's possessions, as if this were a rite of recovery. Emptying wardrobes, as Didion discovered, is a common focus for these would-be assistants. 'Many people,' she writes, 'had mentioned the necessity for giving the clothes away, usually in the well-intentioned but (as it turns out) misguided form of offering to help me do this.' Didion instead begins the process by herself, pauses 'at the door of the room. I could not give away the rest of his shoes. I stood there for a moment, then realised why: he would need shoes if he was to return.'

This is the magical thinking of her title, a form of denial so potent that even when, as Didion and I, you have touched the cooling skin of your dearest love, witnessed beyond doubt the irrevocability of death, you act as if you could rewrite history. You tell yourself that if you but hope passionately enough, if you take better or different decisions, still you might dodge the speeding bullet that has already passed through your heart.

It may be a symptom of this disorder that I never quite get around to reading Devine and Bonanno or disposing of a single piece of Andy's clothing. It's hard to say. For a while, lockdown makes the decision on clothing for me. There's no possibility of inviting Isaac and the band to go through his shirts and suits to see if there's anything they fancy. I can't donate the pant- and slipper-mountain to my local Age Concern, like neighbouring shops locked tight.

Instead, one day I pull on Andy's grey sweatpants. Next I try on his trainers, discovering they fit better than my own since the compulsion to walk mangled my feet. Soon I graduate to the three items of his clothing that his friends most closely associate with him: his three-quarter-length shorts and two pairs of camouflage trousers.

Andy wore the shorts no matter the weather. Photos capture him muffled in winter coats and scarves, the white of his calves and finely turned ankles a declaration of the spring we allowed ourselves to believe would always come. Isaac teased him relentlessly about his fondness for camouflage. The trousers come in different colour combinations, olives and beiges for desert manoeuvres, blues and greys for marine. You look bang on trend, Isaac assured his uncle, tongue firmly in cheek. What the shorts and the camos have in common is a profusion of pockets. Andy loved a pocket – on trousers, never on shirts. The ringing of his mobile invariably triggered a panic reaction as he searched multiple pockets to determine where he'd stowed it.

The other day, on one of my walks and wearing the desert camos, this happened to me. I missed the call and stood in the shadow of the Shard, laughing and crying. Nobody asked me if I was all right. On London streets, people in confusion or distress, already a common sight before the pandemic, are as unremarkable a feature of the landscape as tube stations and red buses. Already many of us turned away, avoided eye contact, adopted the colours of big-city camouflage. Now that human proximity carries a new layer of danger, our survival instinct is grown stronger still.

As it happens, I would have waved away anyone who broke this pattern. Fine, I'd have mumbled, I'm fine, not fully a lie. My reaction had been one of recognition and love. In wearing Andy's clothes, I don't seek to stand in for him – I'm not quite so unhinged – but to feel his presence. Sometimes, as beneath the Shard, that presence is overwhelming.

Anyway, there's nothing wrong with wearing your heart on your sleeve or some other part of the body. I may yet take inspiration from Isaac. My nephew has a tattoo on his ankle, a tribute to Andy of his own design, the outline of a Fender Stratocaster, deliberately unfinished, and, where the strings would be, the number four. I am contemplating something more elaborate: an Andy Gill coat of arms, the escutcheon decorated with a smashed guitar, crossed wine glasses and oysters rampant beneath a coronet of stolen soap and a crest of still-wrapped slippers, supported by dogs, tails decently covering their arseholes. The slogan would commemorate one of Andy's frequent imprecations: 'Cut to the chase'; the motto another of his well-worn phrases: 'You're so lucky to be with me'. It makes me feel better just thinking about it.

The world's third largest belief system, like death, is an absence. The religiously unconvinced – atheists and agnostics – rank just after Christians and Muslims as a percentage of the global population, ahead of Hindus, Buddhists, folk religionists and others, including Jews. For decades we unbelievers gained in numbers but demographic projections from the Washington-based Pew Research Center suggest a series of realignments, with most major faith groups gaining adherents and disbelief beginning to recede.

Any such resurgence will come too late for me and my mother. We face bereavement without the balm of a promised afterlife or ready-made explanation for suffering. We make our decisions about what to memorialise and how to deal with John and Andy's possessions without the guidance of religious rituals and traditions.

For most if not all of their long lives, my parents have rejected religion, Jew-ish rather than Jewish, my mother the product of a Jewish father, Lewis, and lapsed Baptist mother, Ruth; my father a non-practising Jew. Lewis's parents were scandalised when he 'married out', choosing instead of a nice girl from his own community my effervescent grandmother Ruth, a minor star of RKO Radio City Music Hall. As the price of their grudging acceptance of the union, they demanded Ruth cease all contact with her family. Perhaps for that reason Lewis also played down his own heritage. My mother didn't find out he was Jewish until after her twelfth birthday, when a neighbour's child threw an antisemitic slur at her, and her father, briefly, explained why. She would never get the chance to discuss it with him again.

When Lewis died, months later, soon followed by her brother Kenny, my mother yearned for something that might make sense of these tragedies. Ruth did too, embarking on a series of flings that my mother interpreted as a doomed attempt to fall pregnant and reproduce the child she had lost. One of Ruth's gentlemen callers introduced himself as Alan Watts, an ordained Episcopal priest. Just a few years later Watts would find a different vocation, emerging as a voice and guide for hippie counterculture, exponent of psychedelia and Zen Buddhism, the author of many books and a prolific broadcaster. Today Watts's quotes and speeches pepper the internet as memes and clips with portentous music. From beyond the grave he advocates living in and for the moment, for understanding past and future, identity and death as illusory. A YouTube video called 'Alan Watts – Acceptance of Death' interweaves Hollywood film footage of hospital scenes with a meditation on mortality in which he argues that death is a form of renewal. 'Why else would we have children?' he asks, before answering his own question. 'Because children arrange for us to survive in another way by, as it were, passing on a torch so that you don't have to carry it all the time.'

I only hope he didn't drop this pearl of solipsistic wisdom on my grieving grandmother. Watts himself sired seven children. Small wonder that he congratulates the dying for 'making room for others'. Nor can I reconcile his vindication of death with the reality of John and Andy. 'In the course of nature', says Watts, 'once we have ceased to see magic in the world anymore, we are no longer fulfilling nature's game of being aware of itself. There's no point in it anymore. And so we die.' Yet John and

Andy still saw magic, still created it too. They died anyway. I begrudge no one the comfort of formal religion or the more diaphanous spirituality represented by Watts, but I struggle with any doctrine of acceptance that minimises loss and potentially shames the bereaved for continuing to grieve. Watts gets right up my nose.

My mother, by contrast, retains a soft spot for him. She says he was kind to her when she acutely needed kindness. Aged 14, sitting at her widowed mother's kitchen table, she confessed that she wanted to be 'something', to find some kind of religious identity. Watts offered to induct her into the Episcopalian church. Ruth encouraged the idea. For months he instructed my mother and eventually baptised her. She joined a congregation near her home and attended services for the next three years, then, just as suddenly, ceased. Faith has played no part in her adult consciousness, to the extent that she never thought to quiz John about his beliefs. His interest in a church funeral came as surprise, though his daughters had always been observant.

Sarah and I debated religion long before her diagnosis with ovarian cancer. As with our politics, my stepsister and I found much to agree on, even as we espoused different solutions, diverging on the debits of religious affiliation, but concurring on its benefits of community, the comfort and utility of forms and rituals. An enjoyable, if unlikely, evening some years back saw Sarah, then working in a senior administrative role for the Church of England, accompany Andy and me to the Archbishop of Canterbury's Christmas party at Lambeth Palace. I'd recently written about then Archbishop Rowan Williams and the struggles within Anglicanism for *TIME* and knew quite a few of the other guests. Andy immediately connected with the other conspicuous outsiders in this crowd, comedian Bill Oddie and space scientist Colin Pillinger, the trio's mounting hilarity attracting nervous side-eye from surrounding prelates. Sarah disappeared into the throng. Eventually I discovered her in a corner, ringed by attentive men in ecclesiastical garb. 'Hello,' she said to me, 'we're just talking about eternal life.'

She believed, as many do, that death is not an end, but a transition. Some imagine the afterlife as a cross between a family reunion and something like the Archbishop's party, a random gathering of souls having a good time under the auspices of a benign, bearded host. Her view was more subtle – and less comforting as she faced up to death. In dying she anticipated the extinction not only of her body but of her consciousness. Her notion of resurrection was one of unity with God, rather than a return to any individual, human-like form.

When she learned her cancer could not be cured, she admitted to fearing not only the pain of dying but what lay beyond; she questioned, too, the cruelty of the timing. Newly remarried, watching her daughters thrive, nearing the end of a PhD in psychology, with a run at parliament for the Lib Dems under her belt and the promise of a London candidacy at the next election, Sarah had much to live for. Nevertheless, she met her own fate, if not with equanimity, then with grace. Her faith didn't inoculate her against fear, but it helped, as it also gave comfort to family and friends who shared her beliefs.

What stories should we unbelievers tell ourselves when someone dies? Organised religions and disorganised New Age philosophies alike work on the basis of a higher purpose, placing every individual within a unifying scheme that gives meaning not only to death but to life. Take away such beliefs and it isn't just the prohibitions that fall away, the *thou shalt not kill* or *commit adultery* or *covet*; the *woe to the cheaters*, the *spy not nor backbite each other*. If we accept our mortality (as many do not), if we strip away tales of souls and systems, it might seem that our best hope might merely be to live a full span, describing an arc from vulnerability to helplessness via as much pleasure and the minimum of suffering that luck allows. Eat oysters, drink Puligny-Montrachet, for tomorrow, Andy, you die.

Seen through this lens, no death is a tragedy and every life the slow unfurling of one. I cannot counter this drear vision with any narrative as neat and contained within its own logic as a religious faith, but I do have thoughts and, that most flimsy of arguments, feelings.

Recently a younger friend asked for advice. Increasingly she found herself pulled into activism, organising a Black Lives Matter rally, getting involved in local issues and taking stands, often unpopular, on the running of her daughter's school. She neither had time to be doing any of this nor confidence in her voice or instincts. She was already bruised by some responses to her initiatives. Yet, she confided, by-standing and armchair-criticising no longer seemed possible either. However much she told herself to step away from the fray, still it drew her.

Activism is like that, I explained. From the outside people imagine it to be self-serving, an excuse for hanging out with likeminded types, an exercise in stoking the ego, and they're by no means wrong. The benefits to belonging to movements and political parties are social and psychological, and that's nothing to be ashamed of. The core of activism is hard, unglamorous grind, the dull, painstaking work of organising and implementing. On top of that, taking a stand always brings risks, in some cases or cultures physical, always psychic. You will be attacked, I said to my friend. Those attacks will not just come from your opponents but from your notional comrades. It is a special kind of grief, the sorrow of watching efforts and good intentions destroyed by infighting. At times you will contemplate giving up, but something always compels you to keep going.

At its most basic, this something is the realisation about what will happen if you do not act, the hopeless, hapless emptiness of failing to do what you can to tackle clear injustices, fixable dysfunctions. In that sense, political belief systems resemble religions. Buying into a world view and analysis imposes a framework and logic. It gives purpose too – the purpose of making a difference.

This isn't the dominion of God or politics alone. John made a difference to many people's lives simply by offering them friendship; Andy, too, and that's before taking into account his reverberant musical and artistic legacy. Everyone has the potential, in some way, to leave a mark. Applying that potential is what gives meaning to life and to death. It is about caring. It is about valuing ourselves and others. It is about love.

The sixth letter to John

6 July 2020

Dear John,
Less than a week ago I wrote to you mentioning Independence Day. As I explained, 4 July was the date Boris Johnson had decided to allow pubs and other public places to reopen. This they did, at 6 a.m. no less. The day dawned cloudy, damp and not warm but from very early on I could hear the raised voices at the pub on the corner and when I finally went out to have a look, all the outdoor tables were packed with people sitting two inches,

not two metres apart. That continued all day and far into the night. When I went to collect the *Evening Standard* this afternoon, that terrible old Irish pub on the way to the station was full of daytime drinkers sitting just as close together and not even outdoors. This is bound to cause a reappearance of the virus and reimposed lockdown. People just do not care.

I suddenly remembered the day we went to Independence Day lunch with friends in Essex. It was similarly grey and cold and our hosts had decked the table, uncomfortably outdoors, with red, white and blue bunting in my honour and had kindly cooked their best approximation of a July Fourth meal. I came home and wrote a poem, which I have been reworking ever since, full of nostalgia for the celebrations I remember from my childhood; sun shining in a pure blue sky, hamburgers and corn on the cob and watermelon on open barbecues, running races and loads of flag waving. What I realised then and notice even more acutely now is that I miss the sense that being American is the most wonderful, luckiest thing in the world. Not at all how I feel now when the deranged despot in the White House tweets whatever comes into his mind, as hundreds of thousands die of coronavirus and race riots burn down cities and towns.

These are unhappy thoughts, but the main reason I wanted to write to you today is quite the opposite of this. I have been thinking all weekend about something wonderful: how we met. The story of the stranger who bought two glasses of white wine for a woman who could not get served and refused to let her pay for them has done the rounds, but I have been musing on what happened in the forty-three years after that day. You, having fixed your sights on making me part of your life, slowly insinuated yourself as an acquaintance and then a friend. You were an amiable companion over a lunchtime drink but not a person for whom I had ever thought of leaving my husband and children. I wasn't immediately struck down with passion, as you say you were.

What changed? As we got involved in the political and artistic struggle to save one of the two large theatres in Manchester for use by all the major touring companies, I came to realise two things. One is how bright and shrewd you were, how dedicated to causes in which you believed, and how universally likeable. But even more, I began to trust in the feeling of being loved, perhaps for the first time in my life, and I loved you right back.

Things moved on and we found ourselves living together in Leeds. I was holding down a challenging job with the newly formed Opera North and you were still based in Manchester with the long drive home. Our cottage was set up a winding path from the road with large mature pine trees. The Yorkshire Ripper was at large. I had previously lived in a house full of people and I was suddenly alone having left my marriage and my home for a new relationship and job in a city where I was still a newcomer. My terror from childhood at being alone returned in full force. You had lived with a wife who paid little attention to what time you got home and now you found yourself with one paralysed with fear if you were a few minutes late.

At first we rowed about this, but you came to realise I was genuinely frightened. Corporate life wasn't great because you often had to be away for nights or even weeks; these events were preceded by me throwing a wobbly and begging you not to go. Later, when we moved to London, you would often drive home every night if humanly possible, getting up at an ungodly hour to make it back to wherever the conference was being held. You did your best and I depended on you completely.

You were no Pygmalion. You did not want to reshape me in an image appealing to you. You did not want or need to tell me what to wear or say or do. You took me on as myself. That did not mean that we never again argued; heaven forfend, we were famous for it. We were strong characters and we both held on tightly to our own identities. But as the marriage went on, we did become Anne-and-John, simultaneously individual and deeply joined. The very hardest thing I have had to do since you died is to lose the -and-John and just be Anne. It feels so incomplete, so lacking. Yet your approval and support over all those years also gave me the strength to carry on bravely as a single woman, as I am doing.

After we moved to London, we continued to build an amazing life together in the house where I still live. Many years on, your health began to fail. I was terribly worried, but my selfish fear of being left alone surfaced again. I begged you not to die and leave me; I told you if you died I would be suicidal and there was no way I could manage the house and garden. I stopped driving and became even more dependent. You were patient and kind, but you were also very ill.

2017 brought our joint baptism by fire. In May you went off in an ambulance with a collapsed lung, taken first to one hospital and then transferred to another but not home again for two weeks. Shortly after you came home and started to recuperate, serious back pain set in. You had an operation in a private hospital far from home; a return visit to put things right, for a few days' stay, stretched to three weeks. You were so far away that visits took up a huge amount of the day, so I began to visit only every second or third day.

That same summer as an arts publicist I took on a wonderful and very taxing job (a memorial performance of *Les Misérables* by local young people in memory of the MP Jo Cox, on the first anniversary of her murder). The job involved trips to Yorkshire and a lot of pressure. I found to my astonishment that I was coping. You were, after all, still alive and at the end of the phone. And I loved the job.

The following year brought fewer hospital stays but increasing health problems. The real blow landed in 2019 when we discovered you had a form of bone cancer which had destroyed your bone marrow (and your spine). You needed constant blood transfusions. Your breathing grew worse and you relied on external oxygen, which meant moving you to the spare bedroom. The stairs became a serious obstacle and you climbed them as few times as possible. You kept getting terrible cases of cellulitis. But all this time you remained unmistakeably John. You never complained, still cooked meals for our friends, drove the car, painted a little, helped me with arts projects, and guided Pasquale in the garden from a strategic chair on the patio.

You spent most of your final October in hospital with pneumonia but came home in time to attend the press night of a fantastic play we had worked on together over the summer (me publicising and you fundraising), *T. S. Eliot's Murder in the Cathedral,* performed in Southwark Cathedral. Towards the end of November we attended an evening to commemorate your daughter Sarah on what would have been her birthday. I didn't hear you exclaim, suddenly, that you were dying but others did. It was to be your last evening out, ever.

When the ambulance collected you on 2 December to stay in hospital 'for a few days' to clear up another terrible case of cellulitis, I let myself believe you would be back for Christmas, but you never came home again. Even then you had loads of visitors and always seemed to be in good spirits, despite all the tubes and breathing gear. We had arranged for you to spend Christmas at home and you seemed in particularly high spirits when I saw you on 21 December. I left to have dinner across the road with Ian and Jayne; we rang you from the dinner table and you sounded so well and chipper. We all cheered up and raised a glass to your fighting spirit.

The hospital called me early the next morning on 22 December and told me to get over there as quickly as I could. I rang everybody and ran for the overground. Although you did not die until that evening, you were quiet all day except for that famous moment when you roused yourself to shout 'shut up' in the late afternoon. I left about 6 p.m. because I did not want to see you die. Catherine rang me about 9.30 p.m. with the news; I was expecting this but, as I realised later, profoundly shocked. I was watching a very funny version of *A Christmas Carol* on TV and, not knowing what to do with myself, returned to try to watch the rest of it.

The enormity of what had happened did not really hit home until after Boxing Day. The little girl who could not be left alone in a train station for even five minutes; the wife who summoned her husband home from conferences rather than spend one night on her own was now a widow, who must spend the rest of her life alone. Andy's death and then lockdown followed swiftly. After a crash course, I have now acquired a PhD in solitude; as the shock which shielded me at first erodes and the pain of loss becomes sharper, I realise, to my amazement, that the fear is gone.

Oddly, lockdown has made many things difficult but one major thing easier. In normal times, after losing you I would not have had an appetite for social life, for my daily coffees here, there and everywhere, and I would have wrestled with those feelings. But everybody has been isolated, kept indoors and away from family and friends, so I do not feel singled out and I do not have to make daily decisions about what to do and where to go.

Recent widowhood is no more punishing than what many or most are going through and I have benefitted from a huge amount of care and concern from everybody. Also, remembering as you do how impatient I am normally, everybody's life is slowed to a walking pace. Ordinary things take ages and are hard to arrange. Nothing can be taken for granted. I am doing very different things with my time than I would have done were you still here, but I am no more isolated or locked down than anyone else, except perhaps those fools at the local pub.

The sun rises and sets. There are new tiny swan chicks in the canal. Seasonal flowers are in the garden and fruit forming on the trees. The foxes are back in the vegetable patch. Pasquale was here this afternoon and we always talk as if you were there too. He tells me what he is planting and when it will come up and what colour it will be. The future could not be more uncertain, but life does go on. And missing you as I do, I still want to be part of it.

You also wanted to be part of it. You never showed fear, at least not to me, but must have known for some time that you weren't going to make our fortieth wedding anniversary. Whoever took Radio 4's *Thought for the Day* last Saturday said that too many people agonise about planning the funeral and not the final resting place. You were so specific in your end of life notes about being buried next to Salisbury Cathedral; although coronavirus has stumped us so far, it will happen. Your daughter Sarah ended up in the graveyard next to her beloved little flint church in Kent, which she had rescued from dereliction almost single handed. Your first wife Alison was interred in the woods in a casket designed to dissolve into the earth organically. Other than having a Will, the most important thing people can do is to tell those who live after them where they want to be eternally. This is a question whose answer for myself I do not yet know. I must give it serious thought.

You were already quite ill, so may not remember that only a couple of years ago I uncovered a great deception perpetrated by my mother Ruth. When my brother Kenny was killed by lightning at summer camp, my mother told me that he had been reduced to a tiny heap of ashes; as there was no body, there would be no funeral. But a few years ago, I was told by a friend that lightning kills by electrocuting but does not cremate a body. The pile of ashes was a total fib. From speaking to the person who now runs that camp and from records found online in a local newspaper article, it is now established that Kenny's body was carried to the camp infirmary, where he was pronounced dead. A couple of days later, his body was put on a train to Chicago, ostensibly met by my mother. Somewhere, secretly, she buried Kenny. No one will ever know where, but he is not in the family plot alongside his grandparents, aunt and uncle, father and mother.

Quite apart from the terrible hoax on me, a 14-year-old adolescent and not a small child, in the light of my recent bereavements and after more than seventy years, I want more than ever to know where he was laid to rest and alongside whom. Why did she do it? Having lost her only son, why did she hide him away? Did she visit the grave? He was the last bearer of my family name and as far as I know, does not even have a headstone. I have my theories. The camp was only in its second year of existence and depended on middle-class boys from cities like Chicago. A fatality so soon was not good publicity and they may have 'persuaded' Ruth to the secret train trip and burial so it did not hit the news in Chicago, where my family was well known. And the news never got to Chicago and only ever made it to the *Jackson Hole Daily Post*. Having given my brother so little thought for years, I now mourn him anew.

A couple of quick last words in this very long letter. I have persuaded Ian to buy your car. He got it out yesterday and gave it one of his very thorough washes and polishes. He has now reinsured and licensed it. In the garage are stored Jayne's cosmetics until such time they can sell their house and move to the country. The relationship with them gave us both such pleasure and has given me much comfort since your death; it is a joy which I know you will share to be of assistance and to think of the car in Ian's capable hands.

As soon as lockdown restrictions allowed them to come over, Catherine A and the whole family came over for a garden visit. At the end of June, she came into the house too. That's when we moved your ashes to your studio. So much nicer than that dark cupboard. We also went through loads of your things and she left with shoes, boots, camera equipment and quite a lot of red wine. Even more important, we mutually decided she should have your baby grand as soon as possible so, last weekend, the movers came. She starts lessons immediately. In turn I have finally done something you suggested for years and installed, in the space left by the piano, the sofa from the other side of the house. It looks great there, as you predicted, and has made the living room in which I have been spending so much time more comfortable. It's where my Catherine and I meet every week as well as being my office and centre of all the work I'm doing to sort out your estate.

Even so, I felt a pang to see the piano go. It wasn't just something of yours. It gave you joy. I will finish this letter with a poem that I wrote as soon as the movers left with it.

The Piano
The grand piano has left the house
To live with your daughter
As you wished.
For thirty years it sat
Elegant and polished
In the stunning room
You created in our house.
In my direct line of vision
From the desk I use many hours a day
You sat there long after
You weren't available for practice.
The gaping hole in the room
Echoes the cavernous hole in my heart
Where you lived and still live
But where, like the piano,
I can no longer see you.

Love,
Anne

Chapter 9: Love

My mother often reveals herself in the things she doesn't say. She speaks, with an emotion close to awe, of John loving her in her unvarnished entirety. This is the observation of a woman who doubts that she is lovable. If she acknowledges such doubts to herself, she keeps a lid on them. So much she has survived over her eighty-six years, and like many survivors she copes by clamping down on troubling thoughts and feelings.

All these months I have watched her, upright on her sofa even as the weight of grief presses down. When first we began to meet in her living room, I believed I knew her as well as any daughter knows her mother. I could have drawn for you not only the outlines of her life, but quite a bit of the cross-hatching and shading of finer detail. Sometimes she surprises me, but generally I can predict her reactions, her likes and dislikes. If asked, before the fact, how she would cope with the sequence of events set out in this book, I would have answered along these lines: that she is stronger and more capable than she recognises; that she responded to her 2003 cancer diagnosis by becoming less, not more, fearful, and would meet the new challenges in similar vein. She had the resilience to manage the pain, the loss, the sorrow, the solitude. Sadmin and dread tape would surely be the focus of her conscious anxieties.

I correctly anticipated she'd need help with these areas. What I failed to foresee was that she didn't expect that help to be automatic. Each time something goes wrong or needs doing, her anxieties are compounded by the notion that she'll have to barter for assistance. Family and friends act out of love, but from an early age, she has assumed relationships to be transactional. Affection must be earned by doing certain things or behaving certain ways. As a teenager, she starved herself into the approximation of the boyish shape of the dead brother she suspected her mother would have exchanged for her in a heartbeat. Her transformation didn't improve relations with my grandmother. As a young woman, she moulded herself to the expectations of the time and place, leaving university in her final year to become a wife and mother. She still harbours regret about paths untaken.

Perhaps from my sisters and me she got an inkling of a different kind of love, unforced and unfettered. I hope so, but those early years of motherhood were tough. Three of us, she had, in four years. This was supposed to suffice, looking after us and playing wife to our father in small-town Wisconsin. She couldn't name the problem that made her restless. Part of it, at that time, had no name, as Betty Friedan explained in *The Feminine Mystique*. It was the expectation that women should find contentment in making others contented, in unalloyed domesticity.

Old photographs present us a thriving, all-American family, the kind that drinks branded products and rejoices over their white goods. Here's one, taken during my first summer. I'm a solemn baby, on my paternal grandmother's knee. Cassie sits facing us, Lise grins at the camera. My beautiful mother crouches behind this group, smiling at me, almost suppliant, as

I ignore her gaze. Twenty-nine she'd have been, seventeen years into her grief for her father and her brother and her fractured relationship with her mother. No longer did she think about these things in waking hours, but it is ingrained in her, the fear. The people you love the most leave, the bonds between parent and child can be severed in an instant, the Problem with No Name inflamed by the Terrors that Must Not Be Admitted.

My brilliant, charming father could never have cured her of this malady. If anything, his brilliance and charm probably made it worse. In her eyes, he was too good for her. Slowly, slowly she began to build the outer shell of the sort of person she believed merited the love and respect of others. She completed the degree she had interrupted, found projects outside the home. We spent a year in England so that my father could undertake research for a book, then came back a second time and stayed. My mother allowed herself to be schooled in fashion by her newest friend, a skinny Italian. She always had confidence in her appearance, she insisted recently, but I remember her worrying about her shape and her clothes. On our return to London, she got a job in the publicity department of the brand-new London Contemporary Dance Theatre. This would be the first of a series of positions at storied arts organisations and the seal on her reinvention from mother-and-housewife to what she termed 'a career woman'.

Years later, when John introduced himself to her in a Manchester bar, he saw my mother not as once she was, but as she had created herself – and he admired her all the more for that effort of will. He was, in the fullest meaning of the phrase, a self-made man and not yet finished with that building work. Brains and determination had carried him from a difficult childhood to the thick carpets of corporate life, but always he'd nurtured a dream of a different world. Without question he loved my mother as a representative of the creative culture he'd viewed from the outside, face pushed up against the glass.

Yet she is not wrong when she says he loved her for herself. Her work was by now intrinsic to her identity and also by no means all there was to her. John adored her boundless energy and inexhaustible sociability, saw and accepted her insecurity, the reflexes born of fear. He learned to navigate her desire for routines and reassurance, just as she embraced him with his flaws and foibles. Their relationship was never without fireworks but all the brighter for that. Love between living beings is not a stable element, but a series of reactions neither party should ever take for granted. There will be periods of calm, of balance, but the greatest beauty resides in the potential for change.

In dying, John irretrievably altered the nature of their relationship, took away that potential. No longer can his love for my mother develop and spark. She argues with him still – about the mess he's left behind, about him leaving her like this – but waits in vain for a riposte. In sorting through his possessions, she continues to learn of new and unexpected facets to his life, but isn't able to discuss these small revelations with him.

During the early stages of her grief, my first priority was to buoy her confidence in her ability to deal with practicalities and to give assistance where necessary. These days my concerns have shifted. Now I worry that deprived of John's warmth, the force of his personality and conviction, my mother will allow her doubts about her lovability to become corrosive, that she will start to imagine my stepfather loved her because she tricked him into it. He did love her, profoundly and passionately, and she deserved his love. All I can do to reinforce this irreducible truth is to show her love myself and point out, whenever the opportunity arises, how loved she is by family and friends.

This is harder to do in lockdown, which cloistered her for a considerable while and even now restricts most visitors to her garden for her own safety. Lise has regular distanced walks with her, but has set foot in the house only once since the guidelines came into force, when we converged to deal with the fraud attempt and attempted break-in. Isaac has also been inside once, to help arrange the sale of John's motorised disability scooter, and Catherine A once to look through John's things, twice for garden meet-ups. Cassie talks to her on the doorstep.

Yet it is striking how many social links our mother retains in these challenging circumstances and how diverse in age are her friends. She Zooms with a mixed cohort that convenes annually on New Year's Eve and in lockdown began to meet with much greater frequency. She welcomes so many people to the garden that my sisters and I worry about the heightened risk of contagion. The pandemic poses a daily question: survival, but at what price? Populists and their conspiracist brethren answer that question with half-baked slogans. At a recent anti-mask rally in London, a protestor is photographed in a t-shirt proclaiming 'Save human rights. No to 5G. No to vaccinations'. Who knew that it was a fundamental human right to infect and be infected? Selfish attitudes and the risky behaviours that go with them are pushing new spikes of Covid and making me want to lock up my mother for her own good. This would be counterproductive. While researching *Amortality*, I interviewed health freaks so determined to lengthen their lives that they had reduced their caloric intake to the barest minimum. Science suggested this diet might indeed extend their lives; sense replied that it would certainly make their lives *feel* longer, unbearably so. What use protecting my mother's physical health at the expense of her mental wellbeing?

One answer, of course, is that our responsibility isn't only to ourselves; it is to others, to an overburdened health system and a tottering economy. And so we follow the rules and, in the absence of clarity from government, invent some of our own. Recently, in accordance with official advice, my mother formed a 'bubble' with her much younger friends Jayne and Ian. Bubbling gives the three of them dispensation to spend time in either house; they can touch too. Last week, I watched Ian, dressed to resemble a clump of aquatic weed – camouflage he uses to observe and photograph otters – enfold my mother in a massive embrace. It made me happy even as I felt sorry that I could not hug her too. Picking up the pieces of Andy's estate has pushed me into socially distanced proximity to too many other people to feel confident about abandoning distancing with my mother.

My love for her in this respect mirrors the love between her and John, between me and Andy. Love survives death if you permit it to do so. It's a question of loving without touching, love at a distance, but no less real for that.

Yesterday something happened to make me feel the distance. I'd stopped by my local shopping precinct to pick up a box of masks for my mother. If we are reluctant to limit the flow of visitors paying pilgrimage to her, we can at least enforce basic safety practices. For this expedition I was myself masked, wearing sunglasses, hat and Andy's marine camos, and listening to a podcast through a large set of earphones. As I emerged from the precinct and crossed towards the Holiday Inn, I noticed a young man signalling to me. He looked neat and nervous, to a degree that made me wonder if he might be waiting for a job interview at the hotel. Hang on a second, I told him, I can't hear you. 'That's because you're wearing earphones,' he replied. I laughed and said something like 'that's not very helpful'. Instantly, he flew into a bate. I was an ugly white cunt and Muslims were going to rise up against Jews.

So many questions crowded into my head about his discomfort and why he blamed it on women and Jews. (My appearance and Jew-ish-ness, concealed by mask and sunglasses, were guesses on his part or, more likely, not even that, simply bugbears at the top of his rage list.) How much abuse had he endured; which histories and false histories had nurtured his hostility? Instead of walking away, I started walking towards him, asking him to explain, seeking, I suppose, dialogue. People would later suggest he must be suffering from mental health issues, but I'm the one who pursued him down the street. He backed off at first, continuing his barrage of invective, then, as I neared, turned and loped around the corner, throwing a final insult over his shoulder: 'Try running, you ugly cunt'. 'What did you want to ask me?' I called back. I wanted to know.

After he'd disappeared, I couldn't remember my planned itinerary and headed home. On the way, I posted about the incident on Facebook, with an injunction not to respond with racism, lest anyone saw this as an opportunity to pile Islamophobia on top of antisemitism and misogyny. Of course, within minutes people were squabbling on my feed and I felt worse, not better. In recent days and separate incidents, my mother has also been sworn at on the street and asked, by a man she politely requested give her socially distanced space on account of her age, how old she was. When she told him, he responded: 'Why don't you just hurry up and die?' What hurts most about these encounters, apart from despair at the wider state of the world, is the reason I wrote the Facebook post. The insults aren't such a big deal even if grief, in removing the outer layers of skin, makes us more sensitive; others manage to live with aggressions on a daily basis. We mourn because our reflexive response has been to reach for our phones, to call our beloveds, tell them what has happened and let them soothe us.

'Love is... the one who helps you put the dark days behind you.' I find myself remembering the motto of a cartoon created by New Zealander Kim Casali, part of a series syndicated globally. Her '*Love is...*' cartoons drenched my childhood in images of heteronormative coupledom, to the extent that heteronormativity was represented by the childlike pair of bug-eyed, pot-bellied creatures that appeared in every drawing. The blonde girloid and black-haired boy-thing capered naked – they were always naked – across friends' bedroom walls, danced inside our desks, held hands on the covers of our exercise books. They taught us that 'Love is... the day you stop looking back'; that 'Love is... waking up with him beside you'; that 'Love is... when the days of crying your heart out are over'.

Someone has taken the trouble to collect 495 of these platitudinous pieces on Pinterest. I easily locate the one about dark days. It shows the girloid running into the outstretched arms of the boy-thing, surrounded by butterflies and flowers, beneath a shining sun. Her dark days are symbolised by a column of squiggles that reminds me of nothing so much as a different cartoon strip, *Peanuts*, and the character called Pigpen, who trails his own cloud of dirt and flies. Good grief, as Charlie Brown would say. Today I am that girloid, nerve endings naked, trailing a cloud of Andy's ashes. Living love is... being able to ring the one who has your back. Living love is looking forward to a shared future, waking up to your sweetheart, crying for reasons that can be resolved or over sorrows you will weather together.

Love after death has a different quality. Like our flat, eerily quiet, it never gets messy. This is both a point of deep sadness and of possibility.

Andy and I had built, over many years, a transformative level of trust. It wasn't about whether we would always behave well towards each other, but about what would happen when we didn't. We had confidence that our relationship would endure. Like swans, we had mated for life. This knowledge freed both of us to pursue ambitions and projects that might have destroyed a love less robust. He toured and got caught up in the creative process, always a new track on the go, always a fragment of lyric turning over in his mind. My work was similarly absorbing. At the end of every absence, of the body or the mind, we returned home, re-engaged, slotted back into our joint life. 'The thing is,' he told the *Sunday Times* of our relationship, 'if you get along and you know you can go through some of the rough patches, it really is an enormous adventure.'

Asked to name something about me he prizes, he gives an answer that makes my heart swell (and, yes, my head too). 'I think she's dead bright, you know; that keeps me very interested.' Is there a memory that he cherishes from the early days? 'So many,' he replies. 'She doesn't do this so much now, but if she really got hysterical she'd fall against the wall and then collapse onto the floor, laughing so hard. Which I find very endearing.'

He's right. I can't remember the last time I laughed to the point of collapse. In mourning Andy, I lament a lightness that may never return. He wasn't its sole source, but we brought out this quality in each other and many other positives besides. This is something I mean to say to my mother whenever she marvels that John loved her for herself. I mean to tell my mother that love makes us more than ourselves. John's love for her and hers for him changed both of them for the better, expanded their experience and understanding. Their happiness allowed them to be generous; they had love to spare. The same was true for Andy and me. Long before bubbling was a thing, he and I bubbled, building relationships with family and elective family of such joyous closeness as to blur the lines between households, creating intersecting communities that shared highs and lows, buttressed each other. We would have done anything for our extended, augmented family and they for us. Life felt very rich.

The series of deaths before John's and Andy's had already shown up the fragility of this support system. In particular in Sara B I not only lost a best friend, repository of dreams and secrets, but one of the key people with whom I would have taken refuge after Andy's death. We saw each other most weeks, spoke daily, spent many holidays together, including the big ones. Already I am flinching from the prospect of the days growing shorter and the inexorable progression to the series of dates that stand sentinel at the gate of 2021: my mother's birthday, the anniversary of John's death, Christmas Day, their fortieth wedding anniversary on 29 December, and finally New Year. Oh god, New Year. Andy was born on 1 January. For three decades I have celebrated with my love, kissed him at midnight, slept for a few hours only to wake and celebrate all over again to be beside him on his birthday.

So to that clumsy question asked of me by a friend in the wake of Andy's death: 'Do you now regret not having children?' Let me answer with unflinching honesty. Yes – and no. If I could magic up adult children, whom I love and who love me, I would be tempted to do so. I am, some days and every night, horribly lonely. I am fearful of the future. What will it be to reach my mother's age and have nobody to care for me? But to bring beings into existence not because of a desire to nurture, but simply to service my needs? That's *Bladerunner*, not parenthood. Anyway, if such magic existed, the magic to create human life, my first act would be to restore Andy. He was more than enough for me and, I think, I for him, though watching his delight in the company of Isaac and our godchildren, I did sometimes wonder.

He would have been an indulgent father and in many important ways a good one. I never doubted that. It was the prospect of my own parenting I questioned. It seemed unethical to have children I wasn't sure I wanted. In this there was an echo of my mother's experience. She loved us. She had never signed up for the sacrifices that motherhood imposed.

Children would have changed the dynamic between Andy and me. We were equals in ways unusual in cultures and economies that value male participation while expecting women to carry the burden of unpaid labour, the caring, the making things work in the domestic sphere. It wasn't a feminist decision not to have children; the feminist act would be to have them and fight the systems and structures that would penalise me for that decision. In that sense, I regret my choice a little, but only a little. This fight would have surely placed strains on my relationship with Andy that, as a childless couple, we sidestepped.

Instead we formed a fulcrum from which to look outwards, explore horizons, try to create things of value. It is that aspect of our love that sustained us. It is that aspect of our love that survives. His death means I can't call Andy, can't lay my head on his shoulder and cry. Yet his love keeps me going, keeps me looking outward, even in these dark times. Especially in these times.

So we are lucky, my mother and I; we love each other and our lovely dead. Is it greedy to admit that's not enough? Perhaps, but for us, as for anyone grieving, this admission is a key step towards learning to live again. Week by week, my mother and I revisit the past, not as an exercise in nostalgia, but to understand how it relates to the present and the future. We are identifying the elements that remain with us and those that don't, pinpointing the gaps and unmet needs, and beginning to think how we might address these.

This is not without its added complexities right now. A peculiarity of lockdown widowhood is that everyone, bereaved or not, is experiencing with us some of the cold realities of bereavement. Human beings suffer if deprived of touch and connection. A smile, a touch on the arm, a full embrace: each of these gestures will trigger a release of oxytocin, a neurotransmitter that promotes social bonding. Zoom calls, not so much.

The pandemic hasn't just put paid to easy social interactions; their absence is dragging us all down. It's increasingly difficult to conceive of a world in which human connections happen by chance and gatherings at last-minute whim. So much I miss but surely some of these pleasures, at some point, will return. My dreams have become small. I yearn for the chance to watch television in the company of others, to read and discuss the Sunday papers, to eat dinner with friends and not be thinking about the return journey to a flat as empty as a cenotaph. I'm not interested in high-octane events. I was never one for parties and red carpets. It's a better grade of normality I crave.

There have been glimpses already, a few lazy afternoons,

a barbecue, a delicious overnight stay in Hastings, my first escape from London since the turn of the year. Next weekend we will celebrate the wedding of one of my godsons, in scaled-back, lockdown form. He and his family are family to me and when we can once more see each other without limitations, I will haunt their evenings and weekends. Yet social occasions, uplifting as they are, also illuminate the scale of the challenge. Remnants of the support networks Andy and I established remain, but those sections that survived the march of death are compromised not only by external events but by time. I orbit through most friends' universes, but am not central to them, nor should I be. As you would expect, they have other people to see, other preoccupations. The virus has made these delineations sharper, the other preoccupations more pressing, but even if lockdown hadn't fallen like a stop gate across the concern that flowed my way after Andy's death, by now the flood would have slowed to a trickle.

Bereavement beyond the half-year point is a bit like the experience of women entering their unequivocal middle age. You felt oppressed by cat calls on the street; now you are disconcerted to find yourself invisible. You certainly don't want the cat calls – or the *And how are yous* – but you check your mirror to make sure you still exist.

When I consider the adjustment that faces my mother and me, the forging of a new way of living, the analogy I come up with is moving home, not within a city but from one continent to another. Such moves punctuated my childhood. One reason my immediate family, for all its fault lines and fractures, remains so close is that for a significant period we were our own nation-state, my parents the rulers, my sisters and I the sometimes rebellious populace. As we shuttled between the

US and UK and then from London to Manchester by way of a short stint in Greece, we retained our links to the wider world, to relatives and friends at distance, but with each move we had to establish ourselves all over again, figure out the geography and culture, walk into that new school, start making new friends. Each move brought wonderful associations and experiences, but always we were Other, foreign, a little strange. Only at home were we truly at home. If I defined my nationality as I feel, rather than in the terms bureaucracy insists, I would say I am, by birth, a citizen of Mayerlandia, by naturalisation a denizen of Gilltopia.

That blessed kingdom has fallen. Time to regroup, deepen existing relationships, initiate others – as and when lockdown allows. I've never understood conservative types who cling to narrow social groups and habits, and come out with phrases such as 'I already have all the friends I need'. Andy used to chide me on occasion for workaholic tendencies and he wasn't wrong. I always have something on the go, a book, a piece, a project. But people are everything and at the heart of everything.

Again, I am lucky. Journalism examines events, systems and structures, the people who make them and the people impacted by them. It surrounded me with congenial colleagues and sent me, as each successive book has done, asking questions about and of humanity. People are a focus of my activism and of the organisations I've founded. In working to finish projects started by Andy, I have already expanded my circle of acquaintance, if only virtually.

New friendships are never a substitute for old; they cannot mimic the patina of familiarity, the bond of shared history; but they bring something else, fresh perspectives and ideas. It is hard to imagine, but intellectually I know that at some future date

I will sit down with friends who never met Andy, who cannot perceive him shimmering beside me, and that will be fine.

The tougher question for my mother as for me is how to ensure that in such networks as we already have or those we build we are not constantly on the outside, orbiting through. No matter how many or close our friendships, no matter that we meet every Sunday, we are destined to feel alone until each of us is again somebody's significant other, loving and being loved.

The most straightforward way to do this, of course, would be to find a partner. *Too soon, darling?* My mother telephones once a week with a man she refers to as her 'gentleman caller'; it's a platonic friendship but significant. Recently the widower of a close friend confessed, shyly, that he had embarked on a new relationship and I couldn't be more pleased for him. Yet when friends of mine suggest I might eventually pair up again, I recoil.

This isn't a position of principle. I have nothing against the idea for others. In fact I often told Andy that if I died, he should get together with Sara B. Such a liaison would have almost certainly ended in tears, but as they were two of the best chefs I ever knew, they'd have eaten well on the way to their break-up.

It is another concept Sara B and I used to discuss that holds appeal for me: a dream of communal living. She was forever spotting large, crumbling buildings that could be developed into the home we hoped to share, her, me, and Andy and other friends and family members. We would need to pool any savings and persuade a bank to loan us the money to get started, then create and sell off a few flats to give us capital to complete the part of the building that would be ours. This would encompass private quarters and shared spaces. In Hastings, we looked at two down-at-heel possibilities, a former hotel and a derelict farm, and got as far as exploring financing before her cancer returned.

One of the buildings remains unsold. Fate beckoning or structural problems so bad that nobody in their right mind would tackle it? Who knows and who cares? After all, I'm not in my right mind. Grief, like love, is a form of madness, a *coup de foudre*, the lightning strike that changes everything. The similarities are not coincidental. To love is always to risk grief – because grief is always an expression of love.

A letter from Anne to herself

22 July 2020

Dear Anne,

My husband died seven months ago today. I've been writing to him, but this seems a good moment to write a letter to myself. The woman who had never lived alone, going straight from childhood home to university dormitory to living with her first husband and then from him to John, has now completed 212 days of solitude, most of it under lockdown. As everybody I meet or email or speak to on the phone seems to want to know how I am – *and how are you, Anne?* they ask – I decided it was time to take my own temperature.

I try to keep too busy to be massively introspective, but it is hard to stop those embedded hamster wheels from spinning. While trying to get my whole head and heart around the fact that my beloved husband is not here and never will be again, I also am confronting the frightening reality of the pandemic surrounding me, the knowledge that just one stray droplet from a stranger's cough could leave me fighting for life.

And to everyone who insists the pandemic will surely end, will it? Most people I know do not think coronavirus will ever completely disappear.

Whatever happens, our lives are changed irrevocably. Alongside my lifelong fear of being alone sits a hatred of change and loss of control. So, for me, even without personal grief, this is the very worst of times.

Already I have changed beyond my own recognition. Far from being lonely and recoiling from being at home so much, I welcome it and feel rather loath to go out. When I disarm the burglar alarm, knowing I will not go out until the following day, I feel relief and delight rather than the cell door closing on me yet again. I am still very connected to family and friends but am also more than all right with my own company, which continues to amaze me.

But even as I truthfully say that, I am disturbed and upset by the now almost total reliance on life being online. Not only am I technologically challenged every single day, I long for the sound of a human voice or the presence of a human being. Having been forced to have all medical and dental contact online, it was a huge relief to get my hair cut. My lovely hairdresser had no option but to be in the room, albeit swathed in protective clothing. The same goes for my chiropodist. But both told me that in future I can only book appointments online. It seems the friendly receptionist is a thing of the past.

Speaking of things technological, I received a surprise telephone call in late July from a plausible woman who told me she was from the Fraud Squad. I believed her and spent almost two hours on the phone with her and two male colleagues telling them far too much about me and my financial affairs. I got frustrated, tired and tearful but every time I was about to hang up one of them would say, 'You just lost £600; hang up and it will be £6,000.' I took a mercy call from Catherine on my mobile (which was nearby, which is rare) and she shouted very loudly 'they aren't helping you with the fraud; they are the fraudsters!' Of course they were and with her help and Lise's I made all the necessary preventative phone calls and rang the police. But the experience badly dented my growing sense that I could live alone and manage things, which means the fraudsters did rob me of something valuable: my confidence.

A different challenge relates to getting older. For a woman of 86 my health problems are few but ever present and in some cases worsening. My eyesight is fading, and my arthritis makes it hard to type and almost impossible to handwrite. I have multiple problems with my feet and even worse ones with my gut. And my teeth; one fell out on VE Day, a victim of missed dental appointments. I have a persistent stiff neck on the left side which keeps me awake at night and hurts all day. I sleep badly. Because I cannot go to Pilates I am stiffening up all over and losing the power in my limbs despite frequent walks, housework, and my daily 'stair exercise' (dashing up and down our fourteen steep stairs at least thirty times, sometimes more).

And yet none of this particularly shows. I am healthy and sane and the same size I have been since I was a teenager. I am coping with the housework and the heavy work (refuse bags for instance) and the dragging home of groceries and I have plenty of people to help with the things I absolutely cannot do. People keep commenting on how well I look and I do not know whether they are tempted to add… 'considering'.

My eyes still see the beauty around me as well as more distasteful things. We have had a glorious spring and more than passable summer so far. The house and garden look wonderful; I am so fortunate to have the privacy of the beautiful back garden as public spaces are crammed. Some people appear to believe, along with Presidents Trump and Bolsonaro, that coronavirus was just a lie conceived to keep them confined to their homes. Beer is flowing in our local square more regularly than the milk of human kindness.

I did have to laugh the other day. Lise and I walked over to the square with her Podenco, Iris. Suddenly I caught the edge of my shoe and fell, cutting my hand quite badly. I picked myself up, noticed that I was bleeding, and went back to the house to get a bandage. Lise followed to ensure I was all right. At that moment, a group of people who had watched my fall without reacting came over to her. She assumed they wanted to ask if I was OK. 'What kind of dog is that?' they wondered, pointing at Iris.

I am ploughing slowly through distasteful probate and the reordering of my American affairs. I am working on projects. The days fly by, they do not drag. What is most difficult to describe or assess is my grief. There are so many of John's possessions still around me; part of me worries about getting rid of them all and the other part does not want any of it to go before I do. There are still two towels in the bathroom and two sets of pillows on the double bed. I still say 'us' instead of 'I' and, worse, think us instead of I.

The pain is constant but manageable until it ambushes me. Meals for one are the hardest thing as we always had a leisurely and chatty evening meal. When I watch TV, John's ghost, like Alan Rickman in *Truly, Madly, Deeply*, sits in the chair where he spent most of his final four years. We bought the chair from the playwright Arnold Wesker, for whom I worked for many years and whose friendship I treasured. The chair is solid, Victorian and ugly, but I will never be parted from it.

So how am I after seven months of solitude? Better, calmer, and braver than I would have anticipated. Incurably lonely and sad. Horribly unsure of the future – personal and national. Grateful beyond belief for the support of my family, particularly twin widow Catherine. But, and this is the most surprising thing, still utterly recognisably myself. Learning to value and rely on myself may be the good thing to come out of a succession of very bad things. That and not ever losing hope and the desire to live every day I have left to the full.

Anne Mayer Bird

Chapter 10: In conclusion

A common misapprehension about this book speaks to common misapprehensions about trauma and grief. Writing it must have been *cathartic*, people suggest, as if these past months have seen me self-administer some kind of psychic enema. They intend the term not in its Aristotelian sense – the prompting of pity and fear through drama – but as co-opted by Josef Breuer and Sigmund Freud. In a joint publication, these fathers of psychoanalysis set out the theory that patients suffering from 'hysteria' might be cured by unlocking, and thereby purging, repressed memories.

The patients they diagnosed with this condition were, to a woman, women. By daylight I scoff at their sexism. In the middle of the night, sleepless and shivering, I imagine myself one of their hysterics. If only loosening the corset of memory and spilling my guts could bring relief. This pain is unbearable and yet it must be borne. I pace through the flat, forgetting that the alarm is primed. When warning notes sound, I realise I've also forgotten the code. So many shards of the recent past are missing, yet the sharpest of these can neither be sheathed nor discarded. Again and again this fragment slices through the shadowed hours, flays skin from bone. Once more and forever I hold Andy's lovely hand, stroke his lovely face, my beloved and I sharing, in our helplessness, a final moment of unity.

I am weeping now. I have often wept while writing this book and my tears bring not a jot of relief. Trauma, as discussed in an earlier chapter, is distinct from grief, though often conflated or confused with it. Specific treatments to address trauma may be effective, but to revisit traumatic events without such support is to relive them, not to diminish their power. Andy's death haunts me. In service to this book, I have deliberately relived it many times and much else of the seeping past – John's death, the fear and confusion, the swarming what-ifs.

I did this, strange though it may seem, from a place of optimism. My mother and I are focused not on trauma, but on grief; our purpose is to encourage the bereaved to embrace grief like life itself. Still in the first year of what she calls our twin widowhood, we have come to understand that grief – good grief – is a feature and expression of humanity, as fundamental and inevitable as death itself. We grieve because people and things mattered, because we loved, because we love.

We have no desire to banish John and Andy. Here they sit, alongside us in the living room, the lovely dead helping us to live.

Some days we do better than others, just as some days – and nights – are better than others. We continue to learn, to develop coping strategies and, beyond that, new ways of being. We are, cautiously and with a keen awareness of capricious external forces, making plans.

How important this is. The very definition of despair is not being able to envisage an existence beyond the hopeless present. Just minutes ago, I cried. Now, as quite often these days, I smile, thinking about what I will do today and tomorrow, about what I aspire to do. The weeks and months ahead appear as a patchwork of potential. Most of the backing material remains blank and the strips are narrow, a lunch here, a drink there, a meal this evening with Chris, the friend who assisted me with the first tangle of dread tape, the notification of death. The pandemic complicates and slows the quilting; I fear further loss; I expect further disruption. The sadmin still feels interminable and for me will occupy at least another year, but my mother and I are making progress. It is easier to contemplate the future since both of us gained a basic grasp of our financial positions and what we need to do to get by.

I am working again, whenever I can. Covid has decimated the industries and organisations that usually employ me, but I am far better placed than most. As planned, if a little delayed by lockdown, Santi and I have retooled Andy's studio to record not only music but spoken word. There is headway, too, on completing the projects Andy left unfinished. *ANTI HERO*, the second Gang of Four EP released after his death, is flourishing on streaming services. Its vinyl edition, bright orange (Andy's favourite colour), as a bonus includes the tracks from the EP we put out on Valentine's Day. It has sold so quickly that we've ordered a new pressing. All funds from the digital and physical versions will go to St Thomas's hospital, with my gratitude and admiration. I saw how much they did for Andy, how hard they tried, how deeply they cared.

With Andy's former manager, Aaron, I am finalising arrangements for the release of *The Problem of Leisure*, the covers album that preoccupied Andy for much of his final year. Once this is beautifully launched, I hope to extricate myself from daily interactions with the music industry. There are causes and projects in which I would rather immerse myself, the Women's Equality Party, Primadonna Festival, perhaps another book. A different dream of immersion is taking shape too. Recently I conducted an inventory. Had I given up anything for Andy? I identified just a single sacrifice. When first we met, I belonged to a diving club that trained year-round in the chlorinated soup of London's Central YMCA and from April to November dived the coastal waters of the UK. The dives were challenging, often at low visibility and to significant depths. I enjoyed the excitement and mystery, the descent of the shot line in gathering gloom, our torch beams crossing and swooping like searchlights. Slowly, slowly down we drift, the water thickening to treacle, until, at last, the hulking darkness resolves into something monstrous, a prow or a giant funnel or a twisted deck, the relic of conflict or human error.

Andy wondered at my enthusiasm for these expeditions and blenched at the culture that went with them, the late-night drives to catch a dawn tide, the seaside bed-and-breakfasts with their queues for a single, tepid shower or a single, tepid fried egg sliding across cold china to accost a white-edged rasher. These small hardships reminded him of touring. No busman's holidays for him. He instead learned to dive in the warm, clear waters of the Red Sea and every couple of years, we'd spend a restorative week at one of its resorts. Once we dived in the Caribbean with my father, at that time in his mid-eighties. Someone photographed our family group at five metres. My father and I kneel on the St Lucian seabed, arms linked, in classic divers' pose and standard gear, my fingers curved to signal all is OK with our world. My other hand searches for Andy as he drifts away. He glows white, my love, like a strange nocturnal fish. He has disdained the use of a wetsuit and wears apart from his mask, BCD, tank and fins just a pair of brief, black underpants, one of the many he bought from our local market in London. He forgot to pack any swimming trunks for the trip.

Not for a moment during these joyful years did I miss British diving, but I never gave up on the idea that one day I would dive Scapa Flow. The icy body of water, encircled but for narrow channels by the Orkney Islands, is a graveyard teeming with life. At the end of the First World War, a German admiral gave orders to scuttle the seventy-four vessels of the imperial fleet held in the bay rather than surrender them. Salvage teams eventually cleared most of the wreckage, but seven ships remain on the sea floor, eerily intact and joined during the Second World War by HMS *Royal Oak*, a British superdreadnought torpedoed by a German U-boat. Photographs of these artificial reefs show them studded with urchins and starfish, swirling with cod and pollock and ling. I longed to swim among them but knew this would never appeal to Andy.

Now I plan to do so, next year or whenever circumstances permit. In the short term, I look forward to time spent closer to home, including Sundays at my mother's. The forecast for this weekend is fine. We will lunch on the terrace of her local café with Lise. Afterwards, we may watch an old film, *Truly, Madly, Deeply*, that my mother asked me to rent for her. Several Sundays now we've agreed to do this, but always something else diverts our attention. Maybe her enthusiasm for the idea has waned. The plot, as I remember it, centres on a woman who clings to the ghost of her boyfriend to the exclusion of the living. What passes for a happy ending sees the ghost depart, making way for a new relationship.

Such choices shouldn't be necessary. The lovely dead are never in competition with the living. They are part of life. The question for the bereaved and those who wish to support us is not how to exorcise our ghosts, but rather how best to welcome them. All of us would do well to extend that hospitality to death itself. In trying to shut it out, we grant it a destructive force it need not possess. We cannot avoid mortality; we can prepare for its disruptions. In this, the last chapter of *Good Grief*, I will attempt to bring together some of the lessons my mother and I have drawn from love and loss.

Advice for the grieving

So here we are then, somewhere none of us wished to be and not everyone expected. Like the family room at St Thomas's ICU, this space is crowded and so harshly lit that even close friends and relatives appear as strangers. The whole set-up has a temporary feel, of a waiting area rather than a destination, yet none of us knows exactly where we are headed. Already people encourage us to move on. We should vent, they say – it will be cathartic. Then we can pull ourselves together and resume our prelapsarian lives.

The idea is a nonsense, but those of you who recently joined us on these leatherette benches may not realise this as yet. My mother and I know how confusing these first days and weeks can be and we couldn't be sorrier for your loss. There is no sugaring this pill: losing someone you love doesn't just hurt like hell: it is hell, nor are we out of it. To taste bliss is to be tormented by its deprivation.

The pain never goes, yet there is good news too. You will always be sad, but you can also be happy or dreamy or preoc- cupied with trivia, gripped by rage or excitement or any other emotion. These walls are nowhere near as solid as they appear. Bereavement at first shrinks the world to a pinprick. Nothing matters apart from the thing that matters. When your field of vision widens again, you will discover that far from being confined to a single mode of being, you face dizzying choices. Your realities have changed irrevocably. Soon you will see that you are changing too.

The adjustment isn't easy, but all change carries potential as well as risk. Grief, like love, can make us more than we were. It rearranges priorities, grants clarity about what is important and what, emphatically, is not. It illuminates the value of relationships and of kindness. In rendering us vulnerable, it also opens us to new perspectives.

What is vital in this first phase and beyond is to listen to yourself. Advice, including the advice in these pages, must never override your heart. However you grieve is the right way.

Most of this you will quickly grasp. There are things, however, I wish I'd been told, a few survival strategies and practical tips that seem worth sharing. Some are tiny nuggets gleaned from dealing with sadmin. It would have been wise, for example, to keep Andy's mobile phone functioning for at least a few months. Without it, I have been unable to complete some of the verification processes needed to check or close his accounts with other organisations. Speedy actions at the beginning of probate – including the use of the Tell Us Once, a government service designed to lessen the burden on bereaved families by informing, in bulk, certain departments and authorities of the death – can sometimes slow the process in its later stages by shutting off access to records. I suspect this applies in particular to those, like me, dealing not with standard probate but intestacy.

There is a different sort of complexity to interactions with friends, family and wider society. How unprepared I was for this. I hadn't anticipated the pressure to put others at ease or the awkwardness of bringing death everywhere as my plus one. Nor had it occurred to me to devise and rehearse a script for dealing with casual questions. I realised my mistake at the first social event I attended as a widow. This baptism of fire was not a baptism, but a surprise birthday party, twenty-eight days after Andy's death. Its unsuspecting victim faced ambush by thirty friends, bewigged and festive, in the private room of a hotel.

Our instructions were to hide well in advance, to avoid giving the game away. So concerned was I to be a good guest that I arrived as the room was still being decorated and in trying to help, got in the way. As the other guests trickled in, I chatted with a brace of distant acquaintances from Westminster politics. 'How are you?' they asked. Clearly this was not the *And how are you?* of the forewarned, but a *How are you?* of innocence. I spared them an honest answer. For a while, my deception worked. We spoke of current affairs and mutual friends. Then one such arrived and made a beeline for me. 'Oh, Catherine, how are you?' His tone and demeanour alerted our companions to the mismatch between the conversation and my wider circumstances. I turned to them. 'I didn't tell you,' I said. 'My husband died recently.' As the words hit home, I saw them scrambling to review our discussion. Had they said anything to offend? (They hadn't.) I noticed, too, fractional but unmistakable, a recoil.

Few questions are asked with less intent to extract a full answer than *How are you?* After a bereavement, it risks detonating a stink bomb. How should the whole-of-heart enjoy themselves when the grieving move among them, miasmic with sorrow? There is no getting around this problem, but I have learned to mitigate the effect by providing information before it is demanded.

When Andy died, I intended to abjure social media for

half a year or more. Within days, I began instead to depend on it, giving small, controlled updates not to prompt deeper exchanges, but to head them off. Then I started to blog for the same reason. By the time I turned up to St James's Roman Catholic Church in London's Marylebone for my godson's nuptials, more than six months a widow, I had developed a better skill set for face-to-face encounters too. One of the groom's cousins hailed me. 'How are you, Catherine? You always seem to be so busy with your politics.' 'You obviously don't know about Andy,' I replied. 'I'm so sorry to tell you this, and especially on this happy occasion, but Andy died in February.' In a few sentences, I also apprised him of the loss of John and a little of what followed, but assured him that my mother and I were doing fine.

You might say that it isn't for the grieving to do the work of reassuring others and you'd be right. The problem with a hardline approach, however, is that it is the grieving who suffer most in encounters that curdle. It is we who miss out too when people offer too little help or the wrong kind. That is why this chapter also offers friends and family guidance on how to speak to the bereaved and, more than that, makes the case for engaging more readily with death.

A world that embraces grief would know how to respond to the bereaved without being asked. Such a world is slow in coming, so the bereaved must learn to assert themselves against well-meaning but bossy incursions and benign, but ill-judged neglect.

As I've made clear in earlier chapters, friends and family have acquitted themselves spectacularly in their support for me and for my mother. We are hugely grateful to them. The following remarks are not meant as a rebuke to them or to any readers who recognise in this account something that perhaps they shouldn't have done or didn't do that they definitely should. In the blithe days before grief became our teacher, my mother and I both fell short when confronted with bereavement. Everyone does. My mother worries she showed too little compassion to her own mother as they grieved the double loss of father and brother, spouse and son. Since my friend Barbara died, a few days after Andy, I have often thought about what she went through when her husband was dying and how little assistance I offered. I remember a walk on a winter beach, her words whipped away by the wind and drowned in the breakers. Always she kept such a tight hold on her emotions. Just this once she cracked and I couldn't hear her.

After someone dies, the grief-stricken can find themselves overwhelmed by concern. As time passes, support diminishes sharply. It is hard to know how different widowhood outside of lockdown might be, but as restrictions on gatherings relax, society keeps its distance. Slowly it is dawning on me that if I want to rebuild a consistent social life, I have to ask – and in this my script still needs improvement. Recently I sent a message on Facebook to someone whose company I thought would lift me. He's not a friend but had dined with Andy and me a few times, including at our flat. 'It would be lovely to see you and your wife. I haven't ventured out to a restaurant yet but thinking I will. And I don't carry a clapper and bell. Am keen on talking about things other than grief.' He hasn't responded. Summoning up an image of leprosy may not be the best way to coax people into socialising.

Even so, most of my requests, however clumsily expressed and whether for company or practical assistance, meet with generous responses – and expressions of surprise. 'But you must have so many invitations!' Nope. The only thing in plentiful supply is unsolicited advice. This is a special jeopardy for the bereaved. My unsolicited advice to the grieving is to ignore advice, at least if it pertains to major decisions. All too often, the economics of bereavement force big changes. If you are lucky enough not to have to move or sell things or take lodgers, wait six months, a year, more, before attempting to reimagine your life. (And no, I'm not planning to get a puppy yet either.)

Pay close attention, too, to the sources of advice. Are they trustworthy? Recently I dealt with yet another fraudster, the second in as many weeks to set up a social media account purporting to be mine and decked with images stolen from my genuine accounts. This one immediately wrote to my followers, asking them if they were aware of a grant aimed at unpublished writers. The grant, like the feed itself, was a sham, but the pitch convincing enough, given my involvement with Primadonna Festival, that several people engaged with the phoney me and came close to revealing personal data. Isaac engaged too, but only for his own amusement. 'Should I give you a link to the programme?' the fraudster asks him. 'Yes I want lots of moneys please send to me,' Isaac replies. The fraudster provides a link and assumes this part of the conversation to be over, but Isaac has another question.

'Can I ask?'
'What?'
'Do you really have nothing better to do than pretend to
    be my aunt at 1 a.m. on a Saturday morning?'

This fraud did not appear to be targeted specifically at the bereaved, but many schemes are, as my mother and I have found to our cost – thus far emotional rather than financial. She is still bruised by her skirmish with fraudsters. I am exhausted to the core from dealing with multiple fraud attempts and have had to change my security answers and passwords so many times that I'm now in constant danger of triggering the security systems intended to protect me.

The grieving must be cautious, even or especially in their grief. Beware strangers who offer, unprompted, their support. Beware self-seeking motives masquerading as sympathy. Beware anyone who asks you for whole passwords or recites, incorrectly, your phone number, email or home address. They may be trying to trick you into revealing your correct details.

Beware, too, the more elaborate hoaxes, self-described long-lost friends or relatives who turn up, without warning, in the grey dawn of mourning. This may be a con that sees the perpetrator buy their way into your confidence with counterfeit sympathy, only to depart with more tangible assets.

Beware another type of confidence trickster, drawn to death as surely as are maggots and seeking no reward apart from the chance to feast on grief itself. Their questions, cloaked as concern, are designed to pierce the skin. The media has systematised this pathology into a strand of programming and reporting: grief porn. 'It's impossible to imagine how you feel at this moment of profound loss,' the journalist says, voice vibrating with emotion. 'So tell us. Tell us exactly how you feel. Spill your grief and your tears.'

There are many and good reasons to speak out from a place of grief. The friends and relatives of George Floyd and other victims of fatal force wielded by the police, the protestors in Beirut, the Covid-19 Bereaved Families for Justice UK, all these people are using their pain to try to protect others. It is incumbent on the news organisations covering these stories to respect grief. Too often they commoditise it instead.

Advice for those supporting the grieving

Recently, when my mother and I were discussing reactions to death, good and bad, she told me a story. 'My friend Helen took a package holiday to Rhodes back in the early seventies,' she said. 'Her return flight to London was seriously delayed and, once they were airborne, an announcement was made. There had been no time to restock the plane, so passengers would receive only one cup of tea and one biscuit for the journey. The tea and biscuits were duly served and a short time later, a passenger collapsed and died of a heart attack. As he lay in the aisle, a woman leant over to his brand-new widow. "What a shame," she remarked. "You could have had his biscuit."'

This story may sound incredible to those untouched by loss. For my mother and me, it's all too believable. In our grief, we have witnessed the brightest of human brains short-circuited by intimations of mortality, the best-meaning of people reduced to incoherence or insensitivity. Tactless and over-tactile, would-be comforters converge on the newly bereaved. I miss human touch, but social distancing in this one respect came as a relief: no more unsought hugs from near-strangers.

Yet please know this: it is better to try to give support and get it wrong than to withdraw for fear of doing the wrong thing. The only people who hurt me in this period of pain did so either by disappearing or with intent, seeing in my grief a vulnerability they could exploit. The latter types, the fraudsters and crooks, sociopaths and stooges, are outliers, the exceptions rather than the goodhearted rule.

Every letter, every card, every message to my mother and me meant something, the words often less than the fact of making the effort. If you are not close friends or family, it is wise, in the immediate aftermath of bereavement, to message before ringing, as most did. This is not to suggest that the bereaved know their own minds. Without the beneficent food parcels from friends, I would have gone hungry in those first weeks and probably not noticed. Others sent me small comforts I'd never have thought to buy for myself: a microwaveable hot-water bottle, a gorgeous, weighted bed cover, bath oils. My father and stepmother gave me a gadget that has helped me to stand tall – a shiatsu massage pad. With Andy's accounts frozen, my income dried up and costs rocketing, my father also dipped into his savings to tide me over, as astonishing numbers of people offered to do, including some with little or no financial cushion themselves.

My mother and I celebrate the lovely dead – and we have come to treasure the lovely living. Neither of us would have made so much progress in reordering our lives without the support of others. I mean of the voluntary kind, though it is also worth noting the difference between jobsworths and people who put themselves out for their clients and customers. In scrambling to appoint a probate lawyer as Andy lay dying, I lucked out. Mine came recommended as a specialist not only in estate law but the entertainment industry, expertise acquired in part during a first career as a professional football player. Perhaps in the peaks and troughs of the beautiful game, he learned how much it helps to feel supported by a team. His has been a sustaining voice.

Each company or organisation has the opportunity to make a difference to the bereaved, a gentle word, an extra push to get things sorted. Of course, you may not know if someone is nursing a private loss, so how about treating everyone with the care and generosity as if they might be?

Care and generosity, time and skills: friends and family have showered my mother and me with these precious gifts. We haven't accepted every offer, but we appreciate them all. The single most important way to support the grieving is to be there for them, to put in the hours, whether that means ensuring that they eat, listening in silence or speaking to a void, helping with administrative tasks, or organising small gatherings and meals. Deeds not words.

While words may not have primacy, it's really not difficult to get them right. To that end, my mother and I compiled lists of phrases you might want to avoid and those you should definitely consider. These lists are by no means exhaustive or entirely serious, but every entry, apart from the last in each column, has this in common – these things were said to one or both of us, often multiple times.

Twelve things never to say to the grieving

- And how are you?
- Get well soon
- It's good to be busy
- It's good to cry
- You're so brave
- Writing is cathartic
- Do you now regret not having children?
- At least it was quick
- You'll find someone else
- [Insert name of deceased] wouldn't have wanted to live this way
- Tell [insert name of deceased] to say hello to [another deceased person]
- You could have had his biscuit

Twelve things to say to the grieving

- Would you like help with sadmin/organising the funeral? I have the following relevant skills [insert details]
- Would you like help with sadmin/organising the funeral? I have no relevant skills, but I can give you [insert number] of hours
- Too soon?
- Do you fancy a walk/a meal/a drink?
- Want to hang out this weekend?
- Don't feel you have to make any decisions
- Let's meet up regularly
- I miss [insert name] too
- Going through my photos I found these
- Please join us for [insert significant holiday or date here]
- Here's some crackola/soup/deliciousness
- Have a biscuit. Have the whole packet

A manifesto for change

So I lied.

In the introduction to this book, I promised this would not be a manifesto for equality. I realised in the writing of it that it had to be. Change is needed, profound cultural and structural change, for all our sakes.

With the clarity of loss and the teachings of recent experience, I see that our treatment of the living defines our attitudes to death. I understand that Covid-19 would never have overwhelmed care homes and production lines, would never have taken a higher toll of people of colour, of the elderly and disabled, if – to use a phrase routinely deployed to argue the opposite – all lives mattered. Endemic violence against women and girls would not go unchallenged and unremarked if all lives mattered equally within social and economic systems. George Floyd would still breathe if all lives mattered.

Societies and economies are instead organised according to the conviction that only certain lives matter. Yet nobody is dispensable, nobody replaceable.

In the eye of the pandemic, the equality agenda feels impossibly urgent, literally a case of life and death. At this time of numbing statistics and rolling misery, we must assert the value of all lives and all deaths. All deaths matter.

For decades I have campaigned for assisted dying. I still do, with a passion informed by observing, up close, lives painfully and pointlessly prolonged. We should not grant the possibility of an exit from physical pain only to those who can afford it or swell the coffers of a private company in Switzerland by failing to introduce the appropriate rights and legislation in our own countries. Yet we must accept in pushing for this legislation that the fears of the elderly and the disabled are justified. Legalised euthanasia risks being used against them, just as the informal version has been. You cannot in all conscience argue for assisted dying without also asserting the equal rights and value of all citizens.

Here's something else I have come to understand. One reason politics serves us so badly in these areas is that we shy from discussions of mortality. We don't want to think about it – so we don't. This abdication leads to poor policies and the absence of policies and it hits us in deeply personal ways too, not least when someone dies.

I found a good funeral director and could afford his services, but the industry around death is ill-regulated. Today I am writing beneath a girlie calendar published by the Polish coffin manufacturer, Lindner, each month represented by a naked woman disporting atop or inside one of their products. A birthday present five years ago from Lise to Andy, it's quite the *memento mori*, an out-of-date calendar that belonged to my dead love, strewn with dehumanised bodies and the kind of solid-wood caskets that in the UK retail, on average, at just under £1,000 a pop. The average cost of funerals is almost five times that.

Sadmin and dread tape testify to rules and regulations drawn up without sufficient understanding of the realities of bereavement. One example: my mother struggles with the online forms and services on which so much of the work of probate has come to rely. Significant segments of the population are wary of committing personal data to websites; many people don't have smart phones, can't afford data packages or, especially in rural areas, are cut off from broadband access. The first wave of sadmin would be a lot to handle at the best of times – and the days after a bereavement are not the best of times to get to grips with unfamiliar technologies or to discover the harsh realities of digital exclusion.

Probate processes and the more amorphous evolutions and adjustments that accompany them are often more difficult than they need to be. We fail to discuss our mortality or to prepare for death until it is upon us. Imagine if we did both.

Imagine if from the age of majority onwards, we drafted basic Wills, Lasting Powers of Attorney and end of life plans, and set out instructions to assist in the eventuality of our deaths – how to work the TV, where our key papers are, the funeral or resting place we would prefer. An argument against this is that such dispositions and preferences would change year by year. Indeed so, but in normalising this process, we would also normalise thinking about death not as something distinct from our lives but intrinsic to them, just as are the lovely dead.

Last words

We are sitting, my mother and I, in her living room, at opposite ends of the sofa moved to fill the gap left by John's piano. The big room looks warmer for its new layout, its cavernous space made more intimate by the additional seating.

The sofa is long enough for us to maintain social distance as we peer at the mini iPad I've positioned on the coffee table. Finally we are doing the thing we planned, but kept delaying. This afternoon we're watching *Truly, Madly, Deeply*.

Just a few minutes in, and already it feels like a lifetime. The central character, Nina, sleepwalks through her days, unaware of the adoration of the men who surround her, fixing and fetching and comforting her as she mourns her dead lover, Jamie. She also cries, a lot. I'm loath to confess my growing irritation to my mother in case this diminishes her enjoyment. I do, however, press pause while I search out one of the pale ales she now keeps in her fridge for my visits. 'What a good idea,' she says, and gets up to pour herself a white wine.

The film picks up a little when Jamie returns as a ghost. He seems a good metaphor for grief and longing. Our loved ones are constant presences, insubstantial but palpable. Briefly, I feel my eyes well up, then steal a glance at my mother to see if she is similarly affected. Her expression is unchanged, unreadable.

She remains like this for the duration of a truly, madly, cringeworthy scene, in which Nina and Jamie duet. As the pair finish, my mother turns to me. 'I think I'll end up hating the movie this time round. Still, it's better than crying all the way through.' I start to laugh and am still smiling as the credits roll. We are closely attuned, we twin widows.

Soon it is time for me to leave. Neither of us likes this moment, every Sunday a small goodbye. 'I wish I could hug you,' my mother says. 'I know,' I reply.

As I turn to wave, I see John beside her. Andy walks down the path with me. 'Well, that film was shite,' he says. 'Did you have to make me sit through it?'

'Yes,' I tell him. 'I can't help it that you're always with me.'

What will survive of us is love.

Leabharlanna Poiblí Chathair Baile Átha Cliath
Dublin City Public Libraries

Acknowledgements

Catherine's

When publisher **Lisa Milton,** captivated by my mother's letters to John, asked me to frame a vehicle for them from a raw segment of my personal history, I resisted. *Too soon,* I thought, *too soon.* An exchange with German author and film producer **Katja Eichinger** changed my mind. We had worked together in German journalism back in the nineties. Katja later married Bernd Eichinger, the creative force behind films ranging from *Downfall* and *The Baader-Meinhof Complex* to the *Resident Evil* franchise. In 2011, after he collapsed and died without warning, Katja began to write. Now, as I wavered, she messaged me: 'I knew it was very important to write down my memories of Bernd and NOT to wait because he had told me that for writing the script of *Downfall,* he only used eye-witness reports that were given immediately. Same for *The Baader-Meinhof Complex.* Memories shift and adjust and if you want to capture something approaching the truth, you have to testify immediately.'

I anyway trusted Lisa's instincts. She felt that my mother's and my stories and insights could help others but also understood that writing this book required of us a willingness to revisit trauma. Everyone on her team at HQ has shown us care and consideration throughout this process.

Lisa is a co-founder with me and fifteen other women of the Primadonna Festival. She and our sister Primadonnas have carried me through the toughest times. They include Primadonna's director **Catherine Riley** and my brilliant agent **Cathryn Summerhayes**, who now represents my mother too. When I scan the horizon for breaks in the clouds, one of the brightest spots is the prospect of next year's festival, the world as it should be for one weekend, and the chance to spend time with my Primadonnas.

The Women's Equality Party is more than a political organisation. It is a family. From the moment Andy was admitted to hospital, that family pulled together. Without the time **Chris Paouros, Hannah Peaker** and **Sandi Toksvig** (also a Primadonna) spent in the ICU, without their ingenuity in beer-smuggling, their generosity and understanding since Andy died, I would not still be standing. So too the Gang of Four family. I thank – and am thankful for –**Thomas McNeice, John Sterry** and **Laura Allen, Santi Arribas** and **Nunzia Florio, Jon Finnigan, Tobias Humble, Matt Manning** and **Aaron** and **Tomoko Moore**. My gratitude too to everyone who loved Andy and made his life better right to the end. Thank you to **Alexei Sayle** for succeeding where the rest of us failed, in persuading Andy to have a last go at eating.

Some of Andy's oldest friends sustained me through his illness, death and aftermath, and worked with Lise and me to stage the wonderful memorial for him: **Emma Biggs, Andy Corrigan, Adam Curtis, Tessa Hunkin** and sister Primadonna **Jane Dyball. Annie Gosney, Noreen** and **Tim Blair** also contributed in significant ways.

If ever I were to establish the kind of commune described in the book and, by fiat, force the people I love to live there, it would surely include all of the above, plus the friends who have made it their business to comfort and sustain me: **David Battiscombe** and **Sian Williams**, **Samantha da Soller** and **Kin Yung Yu**, **Josephine Fairley** and **Craig Sams**, **Nicola** and **Luke Jennings** and their adult children, and **Joanne Mason**.

Summonses would be issued, too, to my lovely in-laws, **Martin Gill** and family, and to the **Dalrymples, Hugh, Judith, Harriet** and **Ursula,** with whom I have Zoomed regularly and drawn on their expertise as I grappled with the science of Covid.

My own family in all its variegated, patchwork glory has been amazing, especially given the profundity of their own losses. Thank you to **Cassie** and **Lise Mayer**, **Catherine and Keith Anderson, Isaac Deayton,** my father **David Mayer** and stepmother **Helen Day Mayer** and to all the **West Coast cousins**.

Above all, my love and thanks to my mother, **Anne Mayer Bird**. I would give anything to rewrite the history that saw our relationship tested with such ferocity, but I appreciate that relationship more than ever. Her resilience, determination and humour inspire me. Sunday is now the best day of the week.

Anne's

My first and greatest acknowledgement is to my daughter, **Catherine Mayer**. She is not only a sister widow and co-author of this book, but the person without whom I probably wouldn't have survived long enough to even contemplate writing a book. She has fed me, done household tasks, aided me in my lamentable lack of technological skills, fetched and carried, soothed and advised. And she is the only person on earth who knows exactly how I feel.

I must also thank the rest of my extended family for their love, help and support: daughters **Cassandra** and **Lise Mayer**, grandson **Isaac Deayton**, stepdaughter and husband **Catherine** and Keith Anderson, John's grandchildren Florence and Tom Anderson, Becky and Elli Smith.

Joanie Speers is both a devoted friend and invaluable adviser and gave freely of her time and advice. She persuaded John to fill in an end of life questionnaire in the summer of 2019; when he died six months later, that questionnaire was our guiding star and told us things we would never have known about his end of life wishes and his investments and direct debits. She has advised Catherine and me unstintingly for this book.

Sincere thanks too to scholar/author Lisa Gee who, after a very brief meeting at a press do in 2017, offered to coach me. I had been intending to write my memoirs for years but could never get started; with her help and encouragement I wrote them in 2018 covering the years of my life before I moved to the UK. My daughters had them bound with autobiographical writings from my early years, 'What Makes My Childhood Fun', and gave me the volume for my eighty-fifth birthday.

There are friends who have been extraordinary, doing all they can to help me through my widowhood. I must especially single out Ian and Jayne Mackenzie, who have been there to help at the drop of the proverbial hat. Special mention also goes to Elizabeth Haines and to Ginette Goulston-Lincoln, one of the world's best listeners.

Close friends Jenny Topper and Marc Hauer must be on the list. Marc is a probate lawyer who gave me a lot of free advice about probate, including a whole afternoon going through confusing documents and papers at my dining table. Jenny is never far away.

Carole Railton employed me writing blogs for her website for women over 50 shortly after John died and it not only honed my skills but got me to focus on something more than my personal grief. Theatre friends too numerous to list rallied to support me: special mention has to go to **Matt Wolf, Corinne Beaver, Kim Morgan, Mark and Rachel Leipacher and Cecilia Dorland.** I leave out many more but must also include former mentees **Miranda Marcus** and **Dawn James.**

When John left business life in the 1990s, he left friends and associates behind except for one devoted couple. **Martyn and Jacqueline Deane** were actually introduced to each other by John and their long and happy marriage mirrored ours. We remained, and I still remain, close and loving friends and they have done and will continue to do anything to help me in these troubled times. They adored John, as did I.

Gardener extraordinaire **Pasquale Calabrese** took over front and back gardens when John became too ill to garden, although John also placed his chair mid lawn and supervised. A tearful Pasquale assured me of his support and has maintained the garden to a standard which would please John as well as beginning to teach me something of horticulture. The fact that Pasquale had to climb a high wall with mower during lockdown testifies to his loyalty and love.

Finally, a mention of a friend who has rung me every single week to make sure I am still here and whole, my lovely 'gentleman caller' **Ellis Jones.** Even though he lives at the opposite end of London, he would be on my list of people to ring at 3 a.m. and say 'help'.

Leabharlanna Poiblí Chathair Bhaile Átha Cliath
Dublin City Public Libraries

ONE PLACE. MANY STORIES

Bold, innovative and
empowering publishing.

FOLLOW US ON:

@HQStories